THE COMMUNITY DREAM:
Awaking the Christian Tribal Consciousness

Pat C. Brockman, O.S.U., Ph.D.

WovenWord Press

For information write:
WovenWord Press
811 Mapleton Avenue
Boulder, Colorado 80304

Cover art © 2000 by Julie Lonneman
Cover and book design © 2000 by Vicki McVey
Illustrations © 2000 by Marjean Clement
Mask © 2000 Bonnie Capaul
Mandalas © 2000 by Lynn McClellan and Mary-Cabrini Durkin

ISBN:0967842816

Library of Congress Catalogue Card Number 00-11023
1. Body, Mind, and Spirit 2. Community Dreaming 3. Jungian psychology 4. Spirituality

The Community Dream: Awaking the Christian Tribal Consciousness

DEDICATION

To my parents who never limited my dreams,
and to my siblings Nan, Beth, Norb and Steve,
who, in living out their own dreams
have joined in the transformation of the world soul.

TABLE OF CONTENTS

*T*he Community Dream presents the reality of collective dreaming to a wide public, especially to those spiritual seekers who have come together intentionally in a group, particularly—but not exclusively—Christian. But this book is also for anyone who has explored his or her own dreams, and has grown as a person through trying to understand them. Admirers of Carl G. Jung may find it particularly relevant to their interests; but I hope that all "professional listeners," other students of the social sciences, and facilitators of groups will find helpful connections to their clients and their concerns.

Although based on research carried out for almost a decade, *The Community Dream* is not an academic book in the strict sense. Rather, it introduces us to other persons in the places where they gather together. There, in close personal contact, they discover their own inherently tribal instincts. These become readily evident to any of us when we divide ourselves into clans or family groups, when we celebrate our common rituals both traditional and fresh, and when we learn how interdependent we are with other persons in groups that are spread out over the wide fabric of our lives. It is in just these mundane circumstances that we encounter the sacred in each other, specifically engaging with others on a spiritual level. Waking, we enter together our common life. Sleeping, we share the tribal dream.

For the purpose of focus, and out of respect for my own experience, what is presented here is limited to the Catholic groups with which I am most familiar. But my communal experiments and their findings can be readily applied to and recognized by other communities with other characters and other identities. Carl Jung's theory and description of the "collective soul" insists on the existence of the world soul, about which much is currently being written. But Jung further fixes our attention on the soul of each particular nation, tribe, city or family. And it is not difficult to take one further step and recognize the common soul in those more immediate and informal groups we call clubs, societies, or associations. This was made clear to me in my work with groups not included in this recounting, such as a community of gay men in Canada, a poor inner city parish in Dayton, Ohio, and dream sharing groups in various cities. In this entire adventure, I have been led by one synchronistic moment after another, which provided stepping stones among the whirling waters of the unexplored.

In this book I have tried to signal the contributions of many thinkers to whose work I am indebted. I must acknowledge, however, that this book would not have seen the light of day if not for the *dreamers themselves*, men and women who dared to risk a new approach to their tribal soul. That is why the content of this book is carried by the dreams that open or intersperse each chapter. In the first section of the book four major stories are told—stories that are then opened up and interwoven throughout the rest of the work.

It may be helpful to the reader to note that the dreams are reported by the dreamer in the present tense. This is standard practice, permitting the dreamer to be faithful to the "dream event" as s/he actually experienced it. Some readers, moreover, may wish to see the total text of the dream rather than only the excerpt cited; therefore, a *Dream Reference Guide*, which gives the expanded version, is provided following the Notes.

Beyond that, numerous editors, readers, mentors, and critics have given time and consideration to this endeavor. They have helped me clarify my thoughts and think along with my future readers. Primary among these have been Bethe Hagens of the Union Institute in Cincinnati, Ohio; my publisher, Sheila Dierks and personal editor, Vicki McVey of WovenWord Press; William Hood of Oberlin College, Ohio; Maureen Bloomfield and Trudelle Thomas, writers and friends with a keen "ear" for language. Marianne Bosch patiently typed and re-typed the manuscript, bringing as well her sensitivity and understanding of the dream world to this work.

Pat C. Brockman, O.S.U., Ph.D.

INTRODUCTION

What Makes a Dream Tribal?

I am drowning. I die and my spirit is watching as my husband Roger lifts my body from the lake. The body is heavy. Dead weight. Roger begins to administer mouth-to-mouth resuscitation. I realize that I want to continue my life with him. I know Claire is too young to be without a mother. I choose to re-enter my body, but am surprised at the struggle it is to come alive again. I am full of pain as my body and spirit struggle to re-unite. How hard it is! But then, I breathe again and am alive (NJ Past Dream 110586 - <u>Gasping</u>, Mary G.A.).

Mary stood before me puzzled and dismayed. She pronounced her sense that this drowning dream was not merely a personal dream. She recognized that the dream carried a larger significance than that for which her own life could account. The dream described dramatically and directly the immediate moment in which our church community, New Jerusalem, found itself in November of 1986.

The dream appeared on the weekend that marked New Jerusalem's separation from its founder, a separation characterized by all of the mutual misunderstanding and deep hurt possible where there has been a great shared love. *The community feels as if it is dying. Although signs appear that the group has made a choice to live, the community is still gasping in a kind of agony. The membership doubts its ability to continue. The tension between the individual pain and communal reality is total.* This is the dream that first alerted me to the possibility and function of community dreams.

A Pathway Through Jung

Working my way through Carl G. Jung's theories had led me from enthusiasm surrounding personality types into mysteries of collective darkness and light. Jung's reflections on the human psyche and the collective unconscious also triggered new wonder in me relative to the symbolic life. Symbol and sign had shaped my specifically Catholic environment. Jung recognized and affirmed the power of such symbols, acknowledging that his Catholic clients were often less frightened by their inner images than those of more rational religious persuasion.[1]

As I ruminated through Jung's thought, it became clear that New Jerusalem, the community of lay Catholics with whom I was associated, had collected a variety of symbols which catalyzed and consistently re-directed its communal energies. From my studies of Jung, from my experience in New Jerusalem, and from personal reflections on the power of symbols, I began to wrestle with this possibility: Could it be that an intentional community's journey is energized by, responds to, or takes action on the symbols which arise from the community's collective unconscious?[2] Further, can these archetypal images be identified, collected, and expanded, raising consciousness of the symbols that activate the community's life? Does relating to its symbols enable the intentional Christian community to *become* a truly spiritual community? Mary's "I am drowning" dream began stirring these intriguing questions in me.

Dreams seem to appear especially dynamic relative to other symbols, much as a moving picture would be to a still photograph. Mary's dream, furthermore, is reminiscent of the Native American tradition of tribal dreams. It is customary for Native Americans to accept dream life as directive, not only for individuals but for the whole tribe. In fact, we find in the primitive tradition generally, a trust in dreams as *the* reality of life. The Senoi peoples of the Pacific area continue to accept the dream as a central guide in daily life. Now, in the development of spirituality in our own culture, many Christians are again attracted to this ancient tradition.

The Hebrew tradition models the dream as a kind of divine communication with God's people; moreover, the New Testament experience of the dream affirms our need as Christians to reclaim this dimension of the spiritual life. Jung defined the collective unconscious as a reservoir of collective information. So if true for Native Americans and other traditional peoples, why not for us? Furthermore, if dreams mediate messages of the divine, then this is a spiritual as well as human issue.

At times it appears that movements of the so-called New Age spirituality are uncovering Christians' lost experiences, while we stand about in confusion, unaware of the "tribal" treasures at our feet. The community dream projects offer opportunity to reclaim a dream world that has been valued both throughout human evolution, and throughout a biblical history that traces God's involvement with his people. Dreams moved that history forward and amplified God's message to kings, prophets and heralds. Dreams prepared for the coming of Christ and affirmed his word through the disciples and saints who received and listened to his Spirit.[3]

Never static, dream images not only reveal the present, they trace the ongoing development of an issue in the life of the dreamer—in this case the *community as dreamer*. A dream doesn't just describe the present moment of the dreamer's life, it includes hints of a direction into the future. Dreams do not so much tell the future as tell a story that is freed from the limitations of measured time. Therefore, the story's images at times prefigure what occurs to us as a future event, contributing to a broad record of predictive individual dreams. I draw attention to this because the dreams cited here, while generally describing the present, at times occurred before an event that gives them their significant substance. The dreamer who is acutely sensitive to the present revelation is often the one who also recognizes its meaning for tomorrow or for next year.

In Jung's speculation on the collective soul, he theorized its existence, and pursued its characteristics through myth, literature, and human experience. He recognized and named the dangers to either the group or the individual who remains undefined by being caught in mass consciousness.[4] While identifying the collective consciousness as masculine and the collective unconscious as feminine, Jung also acknowledged mass consciousness, the pattern of social ills which arise from the Shadow side of a nation or group, asserting that *to be unaware* of its character is to be vulnerable to its control.[5]

Can a Dream Belong to the "Tribe," or Community?

The purpose of this book is to address the educated audience of persons interested in or aware of the communal, or collective, soul. These persons may belong to a dream group, a religiously based community, even a bowling league—or any group comprised of those who choose to throw their lot together for a common purpose. My hope is to alert traditional Christian communities and churches to their own histories replete with mystics and common folk guided by dreams and waking visions, and to remind these groups of such mediumistic persons in their midst. The ongoing transformation of these groups involves a conversion from stagnation or death into new life and freedom. It is the vehicle of the dream that I wish to reintroduce into this shifting domain. The dream as a means of receiving God's word is a source of transformation and guidance. The religious psychology of Carl G. Jung considers dream symbols, for so long neglected in the Christian community, as pivotal among the established sources of transformation in human life.

Justification that a dream may belong to a community is rooted in four sources:

1. the theories of Carl G. Jung and his interpreters regarding the function of dreams in the individual and in the collective unconscious;
2. the record of tribal dreams and their influence among primitive groups;
3. the experiments of Henry Reed, Ph.D., with dreaming communities; and,

3

4. observation of the effects of dream symbols in the lived experience of both scriptural and contemporary communities.

The tribal dream, in these instances, often describes a current situation, indicates the complication a community is dealing with, hints at ways to deal with the complication, and may give a sense of future direction.

Central to Jung's inquiry was the task of investigating the structures of the unconscious and the role of dreams in revealing its symbolic content. One function of the dream is to warn against the dangers of mass consciousness, the place where a person dissolves into an indistinguishable aspect of family, church or society. Group life can leave persons without a separate identity. Often within the Church itself, members have become so identified with its mass consciousness that they have neglected the care of their own souls. Dreams, therefore, stress that the importance of individuation—the process of separating from the collective psyche—cannot be overestimated. Without individuation, a person's actions "follow the crowd," leaving him/her without a sense of authenticity.

A distinction arises necessarily in evaluating the individual relative to the collective. Insofar as the individual *denies* messages from the unconscious, s/he is swept by its unrecognized power and remains undifferentiated. On the other hand, in separating from the communal identity, the individual takes on his/her unique identity and is free to influence the collective in a positive way. In this way those who gather into community bring the *group itself* to a collective transformation and into greater maturity. Groups, therefore, like individuals, have a collective soul and must differentiate from the larger society in order to live out their potential as fully as possible.

Metamorphosis - Individual and Communal

Researchers studying human community have recognized that patterns of individual development repeat themselves on a larger scale in the life of groups. Early on Jung applied his understanding of individual human development to such collective forms as the national Shadow.[6] He states in regard to the level of collective identification:

> Inasmuch as there are differentiations corresponding to race, tribe, and even family, there is also a collective psyche limited to race, tribe, and family over and above the universal collective psyche (CW, v. 7, *The Structure of the Psyche*, "The Relations Between the Ego and the Unconscious," 147-48).

Jung continues to offer his perspective on the responsibility to the whole that this places on us as members of the human family:

> This widened consciousness . . . is a function of relationship, . . . bringing the individual into absolute, binding and indissoluble communion

4

with the world at large. . . . The processes of the collective unconscious are concerned not only with the more or less personal relations of an individual to his family or to a wider social group, but with his relations to society and to the human community in general (Ibid.).

And on the relationship of the individual to the collective:

Man's individual situation is the same in principle as the collective situation. He is a social microcosm, reflecting on the smallest scale the quantities of society at large, or conversely, as the smallest social unit, cumulatively producing the collective dissociation. The latter possibility is the more likely one, as the only direct and concrete carrier of life is the individual personality, while society can claim reality only in so far as [it] is represented by a certain number of individuals (CW, v. 10, *Civilization in Transition,* "The Undiscovered Self (Present and Future)" 247ff.).

On the basis of this thinking, a number of current theorists have followed by applying Jung's concept of the collective unconscious to very real contemporary situations. Jeremy Taylor uses these principles to point out the social responsibility resting on the shoulders of each individual.[7] The nature of collective persona and Shadow are the focus of David K. Shipler's study of the complex relationship between Arabs and Jews in his book on this topic.[8] Prior to these studies, and on an experimental level, Henry Reed's research with community dreaming became central to my investigations. He began with a project in which a group of persons dreamed effectively for one other member of a group. This provided a first step toward a group dreaming for its entire community.[9] Reed's work identifies the tension between the individual and the communal as the central source of growth and creativity in a community. Like a quilt's stitches that hold together the individual pieces—the shifting pattern, the give and take, the sewing of each one's piece into place—dependence on others completes the work that s/he cannot do alone. The quilt thus has a Eucharistic quality to it, expressing the union of the group through many elements of the community.

In another study involving Catholic religious Congregations and Orders, Lawrence Cada and his associates developed their concept of the life cycles of communities, relating the principles of sociology and organizational development to the path of individual adult transformation.[10] In still another arena, Susan Watkins collected the dreams of a town, focusing on gifts of clairvoyance, precognition and telepathy. In her book she interweaves the major events of the town life—usually the catastrophic—with the dreams of selected individuals and her own extraordinary psychic powers.[11] All of these researchers recognize and relate the importance of the relationship of specific individuals to the larger communal experience, respectively, the nation, the religious community, and a town.

Conclusion

Mary's dream, which opens this introduction, is about the death and resurrection of a tribe. In it the community experiences itself as dead weight. A creative God (in this case masculine), is breathing life into the inanimate body, breathing Spirit into the feminine. A new wedding is taking place. Here is the Spirit re-entering the dead body of Jesus. Here is Jesus breathing that same Spirit again into his grieving disciples (Jn. 20:22). Here, too, the Pentecostal Spirit promises a different and more comprehensive existence as church.

This, then, is a paschal moment in a "tribe's story," the ancient mystery of exodus through the dark canal of a Red Sea birth. The safe womb of New Jerusalem's founding years had released the community to a life of new possibilities and powers, the challenge of accepting God's trust in the people themselves. It is a story of a love which moves through misunderstanding and hurt to a deeper, more mature and more humble love than it had ever known. The passage of this period has been described, enlightened and directed by numerous communal symbols; however, in this process, it is the dreams that have presented themselves as the *new* vehicle for communal transformation. And that discovery has paved the way for the other tribal dream ventures that are described in this book.

Section A

EXPERIENCES OF THE TRIBAL DREAM

CHAPTER ONE

The Dreams of a Lay Christian Community

We are all living together in a summer hotel or summer camp; it is important that this building is suitable only for summer living - it is all natural wood, not painted or weatherworn. There is no insulation, and a vast amount of windows with only screens on them.

There is a sick child, an adolescent, who has a room to himself.

This is a very happy place to live (NJ Dream 60.012690 - <u>Love Above All</u>, Barb G.).

The Adventure of Community

The story of New Jerusalem Community has already been recorded in its collective soul. The members have gathered their dreams so as to more deeply understand their past, to encounter the meaning of their present, and to find signs of what is still to come. They have found that we cannot "go it alone." The wider the world stretches, the more all of us recognize that our planet is just a tiny vulnerable spot on the sweeping path of the universal journey. If we, as Earth, experience the awe and the threat of being lost amid larger realities, how much more so does the individual person who is shoved and pushed about by the wars, the economics, the confused relationships of our times. Nations may provide economic systems, but they are hardly family. Even our families of origin, often enough, are *neither* viable economic systems, support systems, nor the generators of our physical, psychic and spiritual life.

Where are we to turn? Where can we hold in balance our need for preservation as well as our desire to go beyond ourselves as fulfilled individuals? In what refuge can security, lively relationship, and an awareness of the larger world come together to shape an harmonious lifestyle? For many, the answer is in intentional community. For many Christians, the answer is an intentional church community.[12]

The "hastening of the coming of the kingdom," for many Christian communities, is the original force that gathers the group. The urgencies of the times—poverty, wars, homelessness—were highlighted by Vatican II within the Catholic Church. Publicity around these issues encouraged and motivated life renewals in many other denominations, although forms of scriptural and liturgical renewal had already begun more quietly in prior decades. One obvious fruit of this renewal has been the emergence of small house churches and intentional communities committed to living the Gospel among and for the poor.[13] In this way, persons learn a Gospel lifestyle in direct relation to those whom the community has hoped to serve, as the ordinary people of the churches take on responsibility for their brothers and sisters.

How It Started: Conversion and Hope

The dream which opens this chapter points to the founding years of the community. As principal of a newly built Catholic school with a lovely small stone chapel, I received in late spring of 1972 a letter from a young Franciscan priest. He was asking for the use of our chapel for Friday nights during the summer. Father Richard Rohr had been meeting with a group of teenagers for prayer. I had heard of these restless adolescents, sprung from a weekend retreat into an amorphous group of Friday night pray-ers. Richard, who had led the retreat, looked beyond the crassness and brokenness that often were there and saw hope for a gospel vision. And vision he would give them!

In the original retreat group had been a mix of young men, students. Some attended because their Catholic high school required one retreat during their four year stint, while others were earnestly seeking to know God. Richard, whom they quickly dubbed "Dickie," taught religion at a local Catholic school. During the retreat Richard's students had come to believe in the gospel message that he gave them. Before the weekend was over, the Spirit had come in full force, in total surprise, pouring out the mysterious gift of tongues and the more demanding gift of conversion.

Soon after the retreat experience, when the group was still relatively small, a happy burgeoning group of students began to meet at the "Pink House," the home of Rosie Kremm. Rosie, a widow, had heard Richard preach and had experienced the enthusiasms of those who gathered around him. The group met on Friday nights, participants coming in at various times and easily joining the prayer and singing that was going on. After teaching and preaching from scripture, Richard would sit on the stairs that wound to the second floor, listening to one personal story after another. Confessions were heard, broken hearts touched. "Mom" Kremm, too, ministered in her kitchen where a large pot of black coffee waited on the stove for those who may have been partying more than a little before they arrived. She listened with her mother's heart, advised, and encouraged. When the floorboards in Rosie's house could no longer hold the mob, they knew they had to find another place.

Subsequent moves, first to a local high school, then to Ursuline Academy, where I was principal, were brought on by swelling crowds of teenagers from every high school in the city. In Richard Rohr's presence some hidden hunger for God rose to the surface of consciousness. At Ursuline, more and more adults joined the prayer. At first they came only to investigate their teenager's claim to be praying for three, four—even five—hours on a weekend night. Later, they returned, gripped by the fire of Richard's preaching, to hear the Word and to find within themselves unknown fountains of praise. They came to participate, ever so vaguely, in a new sense of community.

Days of miracles began. A few adults were scattered amidst the crowd one evening when a young woman rose and picked her way through the students sitting packed, body to body, on the floor. She seemed unsteady, pausing at the altar where Richard had just begun offering the Eucharistic gifts. Leaning forward, she whispered into Richard's ear. His eyes widened and he invited her to share her story. Rhonda had been born with cerebral palsy. She had endured repeated surgeries, only walking with braces and crutches. That day the doctor had told her he could do nothing more for her. She would now have to be confined to a wheelchair. Disconsolate, she told her friends who insisted she join them for prayer that evening. She came, not so much drawn to prayer as to the loving support that was becoming a central part of the gathered experience.

That evening Rhonda, as she sat on a bench by the wall, experienced a new sensation, a flood of warmth through her legs. She rose and walked toward the altar unassisted for the first time. In subsequent prayer meetings she was to feel that same warmth—first in her arms, then later through her brain. At none of these times was anyone specifically praying for *her*. But she knew that she had been healed physically, a fact which her doctors confirmed a year later. The doctor who had directed her treatment for eighteen years stated simply that she had had cerebral palsy for eighteen years, but now—for reasons unknown to medical science— all tests indicated that she was in perfect health. He recommended simply that she get some exercise!

11

Who is to know the meaning of such dramatic changes in a person's life? We could only wonder, puzzle, search for some response to a God who was being revealed so directly. It was evident that such moments spoke both to the dream's "sick adolescent" and to the "happy place to be." Moreover, these changes pointed to the deep inner changes that needed to and began to occur in each of us.[14]

The church itself was discovering its own sickness. Vatican II had freed its members to name the sins of judgment and condemnation which the church had directed at other Christians. Awareness of dogmatic rigidity and institutional blindness enlightened the documents shaped by the Council. Pope John XXIII seemed to have no fears about confronting the long suppressed secrets of our communal sin. The "new" church after the Vatican Council had a lot of growing up to do. In the high heydays of the charismatic renewal in mainline Christian churches, which followed upon the Vatican Council, the Spirit was launching a new way of being together. The rediscovery of scripture as a force for daily living, the inspiration of a charismatic leader, and the gathering of *these* persons in *this* place began to shape a little group later to be called New Jerusalem. "Were not our hearts burning within us while he spoke to us on the way?"[15]

As a vague and generalized desire for community began to unfold into specific ways of being together, new behaviors were identified that united us with many others caught in the turnarounds urged by Vatican II. We laid hands on one another for healing, young men and women traveled among groups of teenagers sharing their experiences of God's love, and a sincere and effective desire for a change of lifestyle became the center of daily conversation. Some even gave away possessions to those in greater need. John XXIII had indeed opened a window and initiated a new sweep of the Spirit across Christianity.

Winter in the Catholic Church seemed to be past! The dream which opens this chapter revels in the summertime feeling of respite. There is a sense that we can live here all year round! The place is fresh and open, neither protected by facade nor weatherworn as the old Church. We are who we are! We can afford to be vulnerable. Summer camp is a place for kids, a place to play, to waste time together—a favorite suggestion of Richard's in those early days.

By 1975 the Friday night crowds had swelled to a regular 600 persons, most coming to hear scripture preached. After those first nine months at Ursuline Academy—the past summer had never ended! —the group had moved from the little chapel to the school gym. The change in atmosphere did not dampen the religious fervor of the crowd, which on special feasts numbered close to a thousand. Those attending the prayer meetings, which culminated in Eucharist, included persons bussed in from cities several hours away as well as ex-convicts who needed to tell their "born-again" stories more than one more time.

It became clear to Richard and to the small pastoral group assisting him that there was a certain confusion. For some adults especially, religious fervor was supplanting the daily effort of relationship and conversion. It was easier to leave one's spouse at home and get lost in a sea of prayer than to confront one's own inability to communicate or to forgive. A decision was made to discontinue meeting in the large spacious gym and to concentrate on supporting the smaller community of committed individuals.

From the beginning, those who understood the prayer meetings in the wider context of intentional community had continued to spend time together. Earlier, the archbishop had taken an interest in Richard and the teenagers, offering a Church-owned mansion as a place where Richard could live and the teenagers could meet in smaller groupings. These more intimate gatherings were often directed toward personal growth. Like a father, Richard instructed, teased, and humanized. Deep bonds were formed. The natural reticence of adolescents opened up to relationship and service among them. Confidence grew individually as they shared responsibility for the mansion, raking leaves, preparing meals or simply plucking their guitars together.

When the mansion was no longer available, the archbishop recommended that Richard approach a parish where there was an empty rectory and where the school had been closed. The pastor welcomed them, his own ministry emphasizing the scriptural sense of community in a parish with a long deep neighborhood history. Although, for a time, the huge undefined prayer meetings continued at Ursuline, growing focus was giving shape to a smaller core group. Its members had grown close at the mansion; now, they began to make choices for spiritual and economic mutuality. It was to this small parish church that the prayer meeting eventually moved. The happy sense of community is extended in more detail as the opening dream of the chapter continues below.

"The New Children"[16]

> *The only room that plays an important role in all of this large building is the children's room; really, it is the largest room in the whole place, and may appropriately be called a DORMITORY. . . . There are lots and lots of cots all over the room, clothes are simply hung on hooks and racks like a GOODWILL store. It seems significant that the dormitory is comfortable but simply arranged.*
>
> *The feeling is that I and all of the other adults - who mostly seem to be young marrieds still very much in love - have put SCHEDULES and DUTIES lower on their list of priorities than they used to be. All is less important than what takes place in the DORMITORY and the SICK ROOM, which is to say LOVE* (NJ Dream 60.012690 - Love Above All, Barb G.).

The dream image of dormitory is an appropriate one for the way in which the founding teenagers of New Jerusalem embraced the vision of the gospel that Richard preached. In a dormitory everything is shared, or at least out in the open. Life is simple. There is no room for unnecessary belongings. The important early community image of *children* is a symbol of the gospel invitation to be like a child. Surprisingly, these young men and women not only did not resent that title, but proudly claimed the biblical sense of the children of God. For them, it was freedom to be among peers and with a leader who did not place on them the expectations of adulthood.

The sick child in the earlier section of the dream is a high school boy, perhaps representing the young persons who first sought to heal the hurts of their lives through the adventure of community. The habits of discouragement and low self-esteem with which many joined the group, and the similar patterns which their parents and religious sisters and priests brought with them, began to give way to hope and a new way of living. In a wider sense, the sick adolescent speaks to the undeveloped masculine in the Church. Perhaps it is fair to recognize the masculine energy of Western culture as consumed with materialism and the need for success.

The theme of masculine and feminine consciousness appears almost constantly during the dream year. This is not surprising, since this issue has been a central conversation in our times. Carl G. Jung launched it in contemporary psychological terms, the feminist movement has politicized it, and church communities serious about justice have found it touching on most elements of their communal life. In a nobler time, men went forth to slay the dragon of evil; in these times, men often mistake people who are different for dragons, and move forth in fear to oppress and destroy the unknown.

The "children's room" is the most important place, the place of *goodwill*. With great zest kids from different backgrounds and different economic circumstances chose to be together, to tell one another their stories, to be "in love with one another." Community became not only a refuge of acceptance, but a resource and a place to give oneself away. It is a happy place to be.

Once the challenge was made to recognize the call to community, the group began to become more cohesive. Those who felt a call to belong to New Jerusalem were those who desired to apply the principles of the gospel in a serious way to their lifestyle. Community became a place of healing and of service—teenage style.

Out of such relationships, commitment mechanisms began to develop natural-ly. Responsibility for the hundred year-old parish center and only slightly newer school building meant cleaning and renovations. There was, moreover, an immedi-ate neighborhood of tough young kids, curious but defiant toward the new "gang" on their territory. Being with them, getting to know the older folks in the parish, and reaching out to those in the public housing down the street became the check-points for commitment to community. Within a year eight young men joined Richard to form a common life household in one of the buildings they were now renting.

In the next years the term *household* was used to refer to the shared living groups. In these homes all money earned was placed in a common pot. Usually about half the members held income-producing jobs while others worked at the community center or ministered in the neighborhood. This pattern mushroomed at once, so that by 1977 close to one hundred persons had lived communally in twelve households. Necessarily life was simple, but not without beauty. Each house decided its own regimen, which included daily prayer, shared chores, and communal decisions about such matters as whether a member could be supported in his/her college finances. Relationships were central and emphasis was placed on transparency and forgiveness. The reality of the commitment could not be doubted when a young adult would hand over his/her hard-earned car to another more in need. To this day, those who participated in the household enterprise treasure this as the model and metaphor for shared life. Other members tended to move into Winton Place, the group's transitional neighborhood; and soon, married adults began to sell homes in other areas of the city and move into this low-income working class neighborhood.

If the central model for community was rooted in the life of Jesus, it was Francis of Assisi who enhanced the model. The colorful legends that have grown up around Francis and Clare became the poetry and song of the small support groups and households, the ideal for relationship. The exuberant and childlike freedom of Francis met a welcome recognition in these "new children" of all ages. They could laugh and be inspired by a person who stripped himself naked before the bishop to declare his freedom from material goods. They could find hope in a man for whom being a poor troubadour was a valid expression of holiness.

Inspired by Richard's vision of life together, many vowed religious came to New Jerusalem, including Franciscans, Jesuits, Sisters of Mercy, and Ursulines. Some stayed for weeks, others for years, showing yet another face of Christ to the young community. The streets were training grounds for ministry in the case of several young men and women as they walked with Sister Toni, a New York Franciscan, or visited shut-ins with her. Sister Toni was of the age—but not ready—for retirement. Whether listening to those in need or sharing household life with those one-third her age, Tony had a heart for the people. Still today, this Franciscan spirituality continues to unfold its mythic depths as the membership has moved into full adulthood, adding the responsibilities of parenthood to an increasingly well formed responsibility to the Church and the world.

It would be true to say that the teachings of the social gospel arrived early on the New Jerusalem scene. They were inherent in the very foundational days of New Jerusalem. For instance, less than a year after the new community was established, the luxury of the mansion was taken from the group as the result of an official diocesan decision. In response to this loss, the young people stood and praised God with utter acceptance and joy! "God trusts us now," they declared. "Like Francis, we are now ready to go to a simpler and poorer place." The Winton Place neighborhood lived up to that description.[17]

The relationship between Richard and the "new children" was defined by their great adventure of love. Suddenly, God was real, living and working within each person. God could be trusted. Richard delighted in the growth and successes of each member, reminding each one that "You are the Church!" and "Its gifts are yours."

One way or another, children do grow up. To maintain that original spirit of childlikeness has not always been easy for those who came after the original charism had developed.[18] Inevitably, time moved those first young founders beyond adolescence to the maturity of adulthood. In the late seventies there were fourteen marriages in less than a year and a half. Cogent new questions arose as time and economics became limited by the definition of new living arrangements and the birth of children. A tremendous shift occurred over a short period—perhaps six years—as the family unit became the ordinary one, and single persons experienced themselves as on the edge, rather than the functioning core of the community. And as the community became more settled, the issues shifted from the immediacy of evangelism to concerns for stability, children and members who were joining at an older age. The dream image of the children's dormitory had gained yet another dimension.

The Archetypal Father

My three year old son Matt and I walk up to a small muddy pond (facing west). . . .
Matt and I want to go fishing—I observe that no one is catching anything.

Matt wants to wade out into the water—I am scared he might drown from his feet sinking into the mud and muck. Matt goes out about waist deep—I hold his hand. Matt wants to explore so I let him go. I make him wait until I get a long stick. I find him a good strong stick. I tell him to hold tight—I realize if I let Matt go I will have to jump in and get him . He cannot swim with his feet down in the bottom if he feels he is beginning to drown . .

I sense the pond slopes down and it has a steep drop off (NJ Dream 37.102989 - Freeing My Son To Test the Waters, Joe C.).

This was one of three almost identical dreams in which a parent is teaching a child to deal with danger. In every case, the parent demonstrates or leads the child to discovery. In every case, there is some steep precipice or chasm to be crossed. The child is teachable and the parent trusts the child to deal with the situation. One difference is that in a last dream of the series, the water is clear, not muddy.

In his many references to the father image, Jung describes the role and influence of this central parental figure. None of the history of this intentional community could have occurred without the influence of Richard Rohr. He knew instinctively his power as father, teacher, and inspirator. He was unafraid of the Holy Spirit within himself, the "water of life," and joyously pointed out to those who heard him the gift of their own inner power. Increasingly the youth turned to his inspiration and leadership as a great hope for themselves and the Church. There was among them a love for the best that the Church had been and could be.

Although Richard named the Church's sin, a right he claimed for those who love her, he also proclaimed the richness and abundance of her history, influence and wisdom. The Church was known to the young community as a living, pulsating being and they lived in that breath of the Spirit that had brought her—and New Jerusalem—forth. The members referred to themselves simply as "the Body." The Church *was* and is, for them, the people, the Body of Christ.

Rooted in scripture, imbued with the idealism and spontaneity of Francis, Richard stood in that spot where excitement is translated into reality, where possibilities are orchestrated into new shapes. Drawing upon the renewed sources of theology, he began to challenge the then current religious assumptions about the meaning of authority and the role of women. For some in our city and beyond, this was critically threatening as the disturbing implications of Vatican II were made more explicit. For others, the Acts of the Apostles assured that a spiritually free and humanly transparent lifestyle was possible. It presented a model of hope in a world where ordinarily the measures of competition and the lure of material success develop a ready cynicism in the young.

Due to Richard's increasing fame, and out of proportion to mere rational explanation, this humble group called New Jerusalem grew in importance. It drew the spiritually "rich and famous" who came to visit, to share, and to encourage the search for radical gospel living.[19] To be radical meant to live as closely as possible to one's scriptural roots, while recognizing that new applications and expressions must be found for these changing times. To be radical, therefore, called for a global vision, a commitment to the poor validated by a simple, loving and increasingly downwardly mobile lifestyle. Richard was called upon to teach and preach throughout the world.

Remaining always the pastor and leader except in the most informal moments, Richard had little interest in the details of administering the community. He encouraged the members to supplement their growth with a variety of ministries; many traveled in teams sharing Richard's evangelizing ministry. They read avidly and conversed intensely about the interior life, the Church and the world. One local bookstore manager begged Richard not to mention a book publicly unless he warned her. On the day after any reference the store would be overwhelmed with orders! So that pastoral needs would be met, members began formal study and training in spiritual direction, theology, organizational management, and psychology.

The concept of trust in God was presented in the image of a flying carpet. The difficulty of traveling on this flying carpet occurred as the "passenger" discovered God pulling out the threads one by one. With increasing panic s/he remonstrates with God, who continues to pull out yet another thread. The conclusion of the story comes when the person discovers that when all other support has been removed, God is still present, carrying the dismayed believer to safety. Following the presenting of this image, any reference to the flying carpet, or to some missing threads, was enough to remind a listener of the call to trust God.

Living the gospels seemed not merely possible but compelling. Richard's joy in the promise of community, as outlined in the Acts of the Apostles, drew the hearts of common persons into the experiment of New Jerusalem. He was always ahead of the crowd, but increasingly besieged by the crowds, by those around the country who depended on his combined simplicity and intuition to enlighten their struggles with a struggling Church. After weeks of travelling, Richard would return exhilarated but exhausted to New Jerusalem, letting us know how much he needed to be among us again. And the new community entered vicariously into the color of the communities and churches he visited.

Patricia Wittberg, in her sociological study of religious communities, highlights the role of the charismatic leader in forming an intentional community:

> The first way to unite an intentional community is through a strong charismatic leader, usually the founder, who can require obedience by the mere force of his/her personality, holiness, or other compelling characteristics. Such a leader is crucial for inspiring lifetime commitment in the other members. . . . The actual teachings of charismatic leaders are often not as important as the sheer force of their personalities and example. They have a special talent for dramatizing and articulating the common vision that unites their followers, thus inspiring in the community a devotion and sense of mission that can withstand great odds.[20]

Richard's word became a living law. It was alive in the discovery that it is the law of love. Why did this particular man exert so much influence? I believe the answer is in the nature of his preaching, which tapped the unconscious of each listener; whether truck driver or theologian, persons recognized in *his* words their *own* inner truth and were motivated to follow it. Richard called each one to give her- or himself in love to God, to one another and to the poor, but with such richness of metaphor that the message was always bigger than the man.[21] If sacrifice as a Catholic term had emphasized loss or repression, now the members saw that to forego the demands of ego released inner resources of freedom. The creativity and energy available to build community seemed immeasurable. Healing was not relegated to personal healing only, but to heightened awareness of the brokenness in our neighborhood and the world.

Nothing was too cosmic for New Jerusalem! Richard Rohr's teachings clarified the role of political consciousness and civil disobedience in the Christian experience. He reached for the heights and those who heard him were willing followers. The day would come when Richard would say, "Having taught the social gospel, there is nothing else to teach you. I've said everything I can. Now you simply have to live it."

A Shift Occurs

> *I am walking east of the Gethsemane monastery, following a creek and asking everyone I pass to show me "the most beautiful part of the monastery."*
>
> *It gets darker and darker the farther I go into the woods. I look back and many people are coming after me with rock projectiles...One of the rocks hits me and knocks me out. When I come to, I am alone in the dark woods and very sad. I look into the murky creek, and there are two drowned bodies: a little boy and a little girl. I lift them both out of the water and know that they are my feminine side and my spontaneous, free eternal boy. I have let them both die.*
>
> *The grief I feel is immense and lasts for a long time. I wakened literally weeping and with my heart pumping* (NJ Past Dream 001082 - <u>The Most Beautiful Part of the Monastery</u>, Richard R.).

Tensions will inevitably arise in community. Henry Reed names the inherent and central tension of community as that between the communal and the individual.[22] He perceives in this the potential for nearly unlimited personal creativity and generativity, at best, a necessary and happy tension.[23] This kind of tension has always been alive in New Jerusalem. But new tensions arose as families settled in for the "long haul," as members came and went out of personal need, and as the demands of ministry took their toll. At one point in New Jerusalem, awareness of the insistent call to the poor, which characterizes the post-Vatican II Church, had come close to dividing the membership. Richard recognized that this was not the community he had first envisioned. The man who had led our very beings through personal and communal transformation, now felt that the American jungle of individualism and materialism threatened to encroach upon the idealism and commitment of the evolving group.[24]

19

For the first time, the father and the children could not "hear" one another. Richard's heart and mind had been filled with the satisfactions of community but, like Saint Paul, this one Church had become too limited for his message. The members, however, felt the constraints of family responsibilities which had set boundaries on their former ministries. Furthermore, the restless "children" had become restless adults, wanting and needing to take on their full power as members of the Church.

By the time of Richard's dream in 1982, New Jerusalem had become a strong and viable community. Many of the early members had moved away from the community but kept some contact. Many others had been added to the original group, which had grown up, settled down and, for the most part, was now raising families. Richard, the dreamer, had begun to feel more than ambiguity and uncertainties about the direction of New Jerusalem members. He asked himself whether his gospel message had been heard and was being applied. There was an undercurrent of restlessness in him. He felt convinced that he had taught all he could in this place.

Persons in the community felt criticized by Richard for his inference that they were not responding to the social gospel. Hurt and resentment grew on both sides, a sense of trust being shaken, ideals being lost. In the dream, "east of the monastery" represents a new life image for Richard, associated with the contemplative life, a strong calling for Richard at that time. The murky creek suggests that the transition that is coming—not accomplished until 1986—is not clear.

After a sabbatical from public commitments, Richard recognized that the pace which family set for most community members could not contain his own ministry. Beneath this outer consideration stirred an increasing fear that the community had lost sight of the radical nature of gospel living. Facing Richard's disappointment was a bitter suffering for those whose great hope had been that their call to marriage would in no way hinder their response to the gospel. Responding to an inner sense that he had carried for a long time, Richard moved, in the summer of 1986, to Albuquerque, New Mexico, where he initiated the Center for Action and Contemplation. He described his hopes that this new venture would be community only insofar as it supported ministry. He expected that he would be able to focus on works of social action. This is not, however, the end of the story.

One would have to experience Richard's deep commitment to his people and their equal commitment to him and to his vision to understand what happened next. After having left the community, Richard approached the New Jerusalem interim leadership for permission to participate in the selection of the new team by culling the list of nominees. It was crucial to his Father's heart that, after fifteen years of building community, New Jerusalem leadership continue to promise a radical response to the gospel; therefore, the new leadership must necessarily be those who could carry forward the total biblical message. The community, on the other hand, had already spent a month in prayer and fasting to discern who might be called to leadership in this very new moment.[25] Its members had absorbed

Richard's repeated teachings on the nature of the Church. Long limited from full participation in a Church organized around hierarchy and ordination, they truly believed the time had come to take their place as lay leaders in a faltering Church. The grieving process of losing their beloved leader had been tied with disappointment that Richard judged them as less than "radical." His involvement in the community's discernment process seemed to confirm their fear that all power was, after all, in the hands of the clergy. Worse still, they felt they were deprived of the right to face the mistakes which they may have indeed made in their leadership choices. Great anger and resentment arose. Every repressed or hidden hurt inflicted by parents, Church, or authority rose up in full fury and turned the group against Richard. Worst of all, community members found themselves in bitter dispute, one against another.

Whatever the extent of mutual projection, whatever the reality, a chasm opened between New Jerusalem and Richard. For the next three years, the chosen leadership team focused on grief, healing and reconciliation. It took this long to bring their love back into balance. Members faced what the change in relationship with a parent always means: I am now an adult, dependent on my own inner resources, and called to trust that the Spirit of God works within *me* also.

Meantime, New Jerusalem's work of forming family, of peacemaking, of rehabilitating homes for the poor, of neighborhood ministry, continued. In the Southwest, Richard's new work flourished as members of New Jerusalem took the initiative of re-establishing ties, visiting, and affirming his work there. They had been led by "Moses's" vision and formed by his leadership; now, they lived in a more settled land. The vision was the Father's gift to the children. Now the adult community must find within itself the unfolding potential to actualize the original vision: this meant a new call to work for the transformation of the City, even as one lived amidst its daily demands and seductions. Carl Jung would say that the work of individuation had intensified on the way to wholeness. Now they were ready to recommit the power of their individuality to the birth of a newly mature and humbled community.

Dreams Confirm the Movement

It was the dream project begun in 1989 that described and confirmed this growing movement in the collective psyche of New Jerusalem. In Richard's prophetic dream of "following a creek," his transition leads him into "dark woods," and into loneliness and terrible grief at the drowning of his inner children. Even in this deep horror, Richard and his community are united, as the 1986 opening dream of this book records; the community, too, drowns and dies. For both at that point, resurrection is still to come.

CHAPTER TWO

Joseph's Sisters: Preparing for Chapter

What had been uncovered in New Jerusalem's dreaming provided a basis for subsequent experiments. The path traced by more traditional religious groups of men and women, however, proved to be different in some respects from that followed by a lay community that had a sense of growing afresh in the footprints of the early Christians. Both types of communities were an important part of my ministry and work.

Individual dream work was central to my approach to guided and personally directed retreats. Several women who had participated in these dream retreats were also members of a Facilitation Committee in their community. Its task was to organize and prepare for the annual meeting of the religious congregation, its formal Chapter. The Chapter, composed of some 150 members, is that official gathering whose business and actions comprise the highest governance of the Congregation. The retreatants suggested to the committee that the tribal dream concept be put to use as the framework for their August, 1994, meeting. They were now asking that these seemingly evanescent, insubstantial products of the unconscious, called dreams, become the essential aspect of this traditional gathering.

Joseph's Brothers, Joseph's Sisters

I am in the midst of a large meeting of women. It is a meeting of the Sisters of St. Joseph of the Federation . . . from around the country. Many know each other . . . we are all "at home" and have a sense of ease and purpose. Before the meeting begins someone begins to take roll call. Several names are called of women who are not SSJ's and (whom) no one knows . . . they are victims of domestic violence, have come to participate with us, and will be delegates to Rome on this topic in behalf of all of us. Since this, domestic violence against women, is the topic of our meeting, we welcome them and are grateful they will be taking our concerns around this issue to Rome.

The meeting is over and we feel we have done good work. Suddenly the women visitors become little flower girls, age 4-5. They are dressed in white dresses and have flower garlands in their hair. People (not members of our meeting) begin to exclaim how cute these girls are, how Rome will love them, how wonderful they will look as they lead little processions around. I am aware of feeling heartsick inside that nothing of substance around our topic and its urgency will be heard in Rome, that nothing will be asked - Rome is expecting little girls (SSJ 18, 031994 - The Meeting, Janet F.).

The dream above leads clearly into an issue of conflict and misunderstanding within the Church. It describes a federation meeting comprised of "families" of Sisters of St. Joseph from across the country. Here the acting membership knows itself as prophetic, acting freely in the Church as identified by the roll (role?) call. The unrecognized shadow, the dysfunctional community, however, has a darker form. Although angry at the "domestic" violence they have suffered as women within the Church, they have been unaware that they have been reduced to "little girls." The membership is heartsick that they will not be heard. They are disheartened that nothing will be accomplished because of the way Rome, and their own hidden communal soul, perceives them.

Relatively few persons have heard of these women, Joseph's sisters, yet many have heard of Joseph's brothers. Joseph of the Old Testament first made his brothers aware of themselves by dreaming about them. They were not amused at his adolescent ego-inflation. They were a straightforward bunch who knew their role in life, and knew where each was in relationship to the other. One was a leader who set the pace and made the suggestions. One was unthinking to the point of cruelty. Most were jealous of their father's preference for Joseph. Two were sensitive, caring for Joseph and careful in their way of saving him. In their midst, Joseph was himself innocent to the point of being naive. His dreams were his delight and he offered them with sincerity. Much later in life he was to make these same brothers famous by embracing them with love and deep compassion.

Joseph's journey from a youth in captivity to an adult of great political and moral power is considered an archetypal prefiguring of a later Joseph. In the New Testament one meets a man who seems at first in every way unrelated to the dramatic and public person that the first Joseph presents us. The New Testament Joseph is not a politician or great administrator, but a working class man. He is, however, a man of dignity and of justice—if we are to consider his introduction to us. We meet Joseph in the midst of a dilemma: a committed Jew, faithful to the law, Joseph discovers that his betrothed is with child. And not by him! His beloved is

Mary, radiant with goodness, herself a faithful Jew. The religious law demands that he reject her, divorce himself from her. The law of his trusting spirit recognizes in a dream, however, a mystery which he is not to judge. He chooses the dream, not the law, as the guide for his course of action. He chooses quietly, gently.

Like the Old Testament Joseph, who became the savior of his people in a time of famine, this man had no clue that his dreams, his decisions, and his actions were leading him into an unknown future. This man of the New Testament, of the new witness, of the new law, let each step lead him to protect and cherish the abundant life of Jesus placed in his hands. Since then, perhaps as the result of faithfulness to God's word in dreams, Joseph has inherited a larger family. That family includes Joseph's "sisters," whom we meet in the dream quoted earlier in this chapter.

Both Josephs were key persons in their families of origin and their spiritual families. It is no surprise, then, that an entire spiritual line was generated from their sure sense of self and each one's humble response to God's word in dreams. In scriptural exegesis they are paired: one as prophetic model of the saving Jesus, the other as the direct protector of that life.

On a micro scale, I had worked in retreat situations with some of the women who claimed Joseph of the New Testament as their spiritual ancestor. They were members of the Sisters of St. Joseph of Nazareth, Michigan. When they collected dreams from their congregation and prayed with them, the themes they compiled reflected typical religious life issues in the Catholic Church; however, although there were numerous transition images, such as hallways, doors opening, and flowing rivers, one theme stands out. It is the topic of the sisters' experience of themselves within the Church.

If one accepts Jung's premise that each group's collective psyche differs to some degree from another's, then the dreams of a traditional religious community should be *expected* to differ from those of a lay community like New Jerusalem. It is provocative that the sisters' dream themes parallel *neither* those of New Jerusalem, the Catholic lay community with which I first experimented *nor* those of the Ursulines, another traditional community of sisters much like their own. Only when the themes merge with wider church and world concerns did the groups find common imagery. The Sisters of Saint Joseph, moreover, have their own unique charism rooted in the scriptural truth and the myth of the New Testament Joseph, and thus of the Old Testament Joseph. They are linked in that myth with a large group of Sisters of Saint Joseph throughout the world. Each congregation's identity is located in its local church, so there are the Sisters of Saint Joseph of Bourges, Sisters of Saint Joseph of Carondolet, the Sisters of Saint Joseph of Nazareth, Michigan. Whereas each shares in the myth of the "Josephs," each also within its religious family has its own history, its own development, and in a word, its own call. One might *expect* a different communal soul to be reflected in lay groups than a traditional religious (in this case, Catholic) community, but there will even be nuanced differences among the images, symbols and dreams of varying groups of Joseph's sisters.

Old Foundations Go Up In Flames

One way this difference expressed itself occurred as Joseph's sisters in Nazareth agreed to a daring venture. They would dream together. To what purpose? They would use the process of listening to God in their dreams to gain a deeper understanding of their present state, to discover its hidden complications, to confront those complications, and to look for clues to dealing with these complications. Like the first dream above, another dream touches painfully on their relationship with the Church.

> *Chris and I are setting up for a service in an old church. We need something from the basement. The staircase leading down is very elaborate and long, made of hand-carved wood. Under this staircase is a storage room filled with used clothing and supplies. I notice a small flame inside on the shelf and call out, "There's a fire in here and its beginning to spread." I run and get a bucket of water, but it doesn't put out the flames. I am beginning to feel distress and panic.*
>
> *Going to a wall phone nearby I dial . . . but it's a misdial. Finally I get someone who is calm and takes the information from me, promising to send a fire truck immediately. I start to race up the long staircase now very hot and smoky.*
>
> *I stop to pray for calm—a quiet confidence comes over me. I get the people's attention and say, "A fire has broken out in the basement. You have time to get your coat and a chair if you wish to leave by the front exit." Everyone gets out safely and gathers outdoors. I go to tell Father X. that the church hall is on fire. He responds, "All that gorgeous wood. It can never be replaced." I feel angry that he seems more concerned with the staircase . . . than about the peoples' safety. Then he adds, "I'll never store all that stuff for the poor again. They will have to go someplace else." I'm even angrier now and disgusted by his lack of empathy. The firefighters report the entire foundation has been destroyed* (SSJ 43, 031994 - Old Foundations Go Up In Flames, Beth P.).

The dreamer feels that the dream points to the significance of changing times. She experiences the fire as Spirit-sent and purifying. Even things of beauty must be let go of. The staircase seems extravagant and out of place, but the needs of God's people matter. Distress and panic are the first reaction to the loss of precious memories and tradition stored in the collective and individual unconscious of the group. What is no longer usable from the basement is burned, even though the staircase was once solid, beautiful and provided a way to God. The basement in many dreams is the place of the unconscious, where memories, tradition, even prayer, change with time and age. "Used clothes and supplies" of the past are stored within the unconscious: the former roles and former resources of religious women are no longer usable. The community membership has "gone to the wall" in its effort to save its heritage and traditions.

Prayer brings the necessary focus and confidence to deal with the situation. The basic identity and the basic support of the group are alone salvaged, appearing as "the coat and chair." The people leave by the front exit, a sign they have no need to apologize for not being able to save what is now gone. If the institutional aspect of the Congregation, symbolized by Father X., seems unconcerned with the loss, the firefighter aspect of the communal membership is working to save what is valuable. A just anger remains at the lack of empathy with the poor. The honest conclusion, however, is that the entire foundation—all that formerly was depended upon—has been destroyed. If that is true, then the group must doubtless use fresh approaches to the renewal and rebuilding of their religious life.

One must consider the ordinary approach to the religious community's annual Chapters to appreciate this decision to take a different approach. Especially since Vatican II, Chapters have become forums for change: practical, well-discerned, necessary change. Well organized meetings have resulted in the radical rejection of outdated images of religious life, the tearing down of motherhouses rich in tradition, the selling of property no longer at the service of ministries, the re-investment of monies—all of this in an effort to return to the groups' original gospel mission. In the process of this highly fruitful re-shaping of old forms, however, it has often been the moments of deep prayer together, the shared grief of confusion and loss, the exultant discovery of new life and energy that have propelled new undertakings. A spirit of unity and joy has appeared not so much with the logic or functional necessities of change, as by an accompanying shared experience—not always of shared *minds*—but of profound brotherhood or sisterhood. By choosing to dream together, Joseph's sisters had dared to choose the latter approach to their Chapter meeting.

From Dream Education to Chapter Event

It was fall of 1993 when the Chapter Facilitation Committee decided to incorporate a dream design project into their preparation and gathering of August, 1994. I agreed to facilitate and, working together, we developed a community project open to all of their three hundred plus members. It would include educating those who wished to participate in the dream project, a designated but not limited dream night, and a "how to" process for collecting images, discerning patterns, and identifying themes. All would culminate in a Chapter event which would be explorative, directional, and celebrative, but only after months of the sisters entering into the symbols of their past, present and future.

I set up a small tent on the grounds of (the) College . . . I think I will spend the night in the tent. During the day I am walking through the hallway past the Georgian Room and the Walnut Room. . . . Then I continue to walk back outside.
There has been a flood. Everything is covered with . . . water, clear, very still water. I go back to the place where my tent had been, approaching it from the

motherhouse direction. The tent is floating on top of the water, so I wade up to it, pick it up above the water, shake it out and begin to fold it up. The water is so clear that I can see the ground easily. So, with my feet, I'm trying to locate the stakes from the tent. Someone, a boy or young man, comes up to me to help me. I ask him about the contents of the tent, my belongings. He tells me there was noth-ing else, then says there <u>was</u> a bag with some things found floating in the area.

I am very aware of how clear the water is, and am not afraid of things being destroyed by the water. I can see the green grass and other plants under the water, and again with my bare feet, I search for the stakes from the tent (SSJ 56, 022094 - <u>The Flood</u>, Sue McC.).

Again, images of destruction! But here is a sense of camping out, suggesting impermanence and exploration. Nothing is done without reviewing the spaces the membership has known from the past. First the community has had to walk past the beauty of the past before going down into the waters of life, then peering into the place of reflection, the place where everything becomes clear. The flood water is washing away debris. They must "feel" their way through this overwhelming time, unafraid even as their view of their circumstances remains above the waters of the unconscious. They must let go of their fragile protection, the "tent," and its belongings, as well as the "bag," the motherhouse womb as they have known it. The dreamer comments that in the dream she is not afraid of things being destroyed, rather there is a sense of search and hopeful excitement. In fact, by looking into the water "they" discover signs of new life, the green grass. Representing the community, she continues to search with her bare feet, providing an image of seeking new grounding. This freedom and openness make it possible to feel around for the "stakes," which can hold the tent steady; however, the very stakes which ground their dwelling, get pulled up when it is time to move on. The tent and stakes are, therefore, symbolic reminders of impermanence.

Finally, in this dream of Joseph's sisters, it is notable that a boy or young man assists the community. The masculine principle gives guidance in its spirit of objec-tivity and detachment. There is an added sense of collaboration. This masculine presence appeared repeatedly in various forms throughout the whole collection of dreams, becoming a strong theme inviting the sisters to consider this factor of their generative power within the Church and the world beyond.

A knock is heard at the door—it is evening and dark. We ask the person who goes to the door if she would like someone to go with her. When she opens the door a stranger asks for something to eat. . . . Before long she has a table set up for the person and herself. Seated at the table is a middle-aged man, nicely dressed in a tweed suit and with combed hair. Before him is a plate of hot mixed vegetables, potatoes, etc.

Looking out of a window, I spot an animal. I go out to get a closer look at him. Much to my surprise I discover it is a bear. Naturally I run back into the house. Before long I can see a small bear wandering outside looking for its mother.

That same night I have a beaded lamp which needs repair. Very carefully, strand by strand, I try to remove the old ones for new ones. As I try to keep things in order, another person is working on something next to me. Her things are getting mixed up with my project (SSJ 23, 031994 - <u>Welcoming the Stranger</u>, Irene P.).

Hospitality is the core gift and grace of Joseph's sisters; nevertheless, they are fearful of what is outside of "the house," (that is, outside of the Congregation). Do they fear finding out what the bear is about? Who is the stranger who needs help? Perhaps the Christ who often comes disguised as a stranger. Perhaps themselves!

The bear may well be an unrecognized shadow aspect of the congregation—something about themselves both to be sought and to be feared. Are they running from this instinctual self, only seeing the vulnerable little bear, the new life, from inside looking out? They need to pursue and to search out this bear, to note that this *ursa*, the caring mother of mythology, is *outside* the house. Secondly, they may need to remember that the bear is an animal that is able to hibernate successfully when the weather is cold and food is scarce, a fortunate metaphor of religious life over the past 35 years. Thirdly, on emerging from hibernation, the bear knows instinctively which plants cleanse the digestive system after months of no food. Could this dream provide an image of the Congregation beginning to emerge from hibernation?

The next scene of this dream shifts images. Old strands of life are removed and carefully replaced, a process calling for a certain amount of order, but which is impossible to assure. Removing strands may speak to simplifying the communal lifestyle, making changes in the externals of their energy source. But they are not doing this alone. Another dream provides assurance and confirms the image of new life:

I am with a group of people. We are going on a journey. Some are walking. Others are on bikes. Along the way there are small obstacles in our path, but nothing serious that hinders our advancement until we come to a large amount of water. I tell the group that this will not stop us. I plunge ahead with my bike and discover that the pond is very deep. I am immersed bike and all into the water (SSJ 1, 031994 - <u>The Plunge</u>, Mary Rita S.).

The dreamer sees the sisters as a ragtag little band with leaders who encourage them to risk the journey of faith and new life. The pond and immersion indicate a baptism. The obstacles—first small, then deep—attest to their transformation from things that matter little to deeper things. There are feelings of fear, trust, anxiety, then courage, many of the same feelings engendered by the story of Jesus coming to the apostles over the water.

For eleven months after the decision of the sisters to be led in a dream process, they went through an education phase which consisted of cluster group meetings.

Each sister received printed material and a teaching tape. Directions were given for the entire process and a calendar was set up by the committee. Dreaming was focused on March 19, the feast of Saint Joseph, but as time went on the dreams took their own course and many arose on a different schedule!

Training of facilitators for the discernment meetings followed. Twenty sisters with experience in group work offered their services and preparations began for the larger meetings. On two days planned for discernment of the dreams, one hundred sisters showed up either in Detroit or at the motherhouse in Nazareth. From working and playing with images and patterns discovered in the discernment, thirty-four major themes arose. (Details of this discernment process are described in Chapter Eight, as the process developed more polish with each new experimental group.)

Relationship with the Church continued to be a central theme:

> *I dreamt of two women whose hands have been cut off—in one instance, both hands. What is significant to me is that both women remain gracious, capable and vivacious. They are not essentially changed. They continue to be who they are and do not allow this amputation to affect their essence* (SSJ 9, 031694 - <u>The Sister</u>, Bernie G.).

The Handless Maiden, an old fairy tale currently returning to attention, appears relatively unchanged in this sister's dream. In the fairy tale the maiden is able to work out her destiny and finally have her hands restored. Hands frequently refer to the work of our hands, therefore, to roles and ministry. This is a kind of Cinderella image, in which the demeaned step-daughter is put to work in doing the most menial of tasks, not an inaccurate image of religious women who have with great graciousness taken on arduous and difficult tasks of salvation, a hidden priesthood. A theme statement reads: "Many of the sisters' dreams describe the pain and emotional violence experienced at the hands of the institutional church. An atmosphere of tension and disappointment accompanied images of priests who are immature and dysfunctional; on the other hand, supportive or radiantly peaceful priests brought joy and confidence."

The theme reveals the difficult relationship of women ministers within the institutional Catholic church, where many feel "cut off" from their own gifts and capacities. Another layer of meaning, often lost or ignored even by experienced dreamers, is equally valid but more nuanced. One must always remember that the dream is a projection of the communal soul. It may become a less effective vehicle of transformation if the sisters deny that *they* are both the immature and dysfunctional priests as well as the supportive and radiant ones. The theme, Our Authority, Our Priesthood, as in the domestic violence dream, appears in *seventeen* dreams, indicating its importance. The community has cut off, or permitted others to cut off their full capacity. The coming to consciousness of this truth now becomes a call to action and to changed behavior. So themes surfacing through dream repetitions begin to show patterns, both challenging and consoling. The handless maiden dream became one of those referenced under the theme: Our Authority, Our Priesthood.

It becomes apparent that the dream symbols, from quite different sisters, clustered in groups to form overall patterns, or themes. These themes cut across the separate dream texts, and across the realities of their religious communal life. Some older or shyer members had come tentatively, long after the project began, to ask if "perhaps . . . maybe . . . possibly . . ." their own dreams had a contribution to make to the community's view of itself. Often enough, these modest persons brought a succinct yet profound dream which pierced through the heaviness of some of the more complex dreams. One sister received and shared the following dream with great delight.

> *I am in Nazareth Holy Family Chapel. I feel full of joy and exaltation. A cere-*
> *mony is happening—much clergy is here. Chapel is filled to capacity, even the*
> *standing room packed with people, I don't recognize most of the people here. A*
> *bishop in full garb sits in front in silence. A long row of women in white robes are*
> *kneeling in front of the bishop. The bishop begins to speak . . .* (SSJ 76, 031894 -
> A Celebration of Joy, Loretto R.).

This type of dream opens a window of light and hope. The happy and wise dreamer had recently attended the ordination of a woman in the Episcopal Church and had talked at length about it to friends. The memory arises in new form as the dream occurs two nights in a row. Now the ordination is happening here in their convent home! The pain of other "Church" dreams is somewhat assuaged by this happy occasion. The discerners recognize that they are waiting for their own masculine spirit, still silent, to celebrate and ordain their inner feminine power. On another level, the dream is claimed as a prophetic promise of the ordination of women in the Catholic community. The dreamer is delighted!

Another example offers the kind of imagery that comes from deep in the instinctual nature of the dreamer. This is a waking image that arose in meditation as the sister focused on the design of a tabernacle:

> *I see four animals with the big eyes of a frog or owl, a cool cat, fox or wolf,*
> *and a happy dog with soft hair. . . . They are upside down* (SSJ 39, 031994 - Life
> and Death Through Animals, Pat W.).

The dreamer is being drawn into—transformed into—the images of the animals. There are accompanying feelings of acceptance, anticipation and longing. The image is more blurred and confusing than the feelings, related as they are to the gut, instinctual level to which these animals refer. Located as this image is, almost sprung from the tabernacle—the Christ-place of presence among us—one conjectures whether these are Christ-images, an identification with Christ. After all, if scripture presents Christ variously as lion, hen, or lamb, then we have something to consider from the archetypal study of the animals of this communal image. In the wider scope of archetype, both the positive and negative aspects of each animal are to be considered, expressing the Christ-self of the community on one hand and the dark shadow-self on the other.[26] In Christian symbology the owl often appears to indicate that Christ died to give light to those in darkness. An air animal, it calls us to meditation, night silence, wisdom, *or* warns of calamity, death and sickness. The frog, a water animal, represents the generative principle and inquisitiveness (those big eyes!), as well as vain and indiscreet opinions. In the case of the land animals, both the untamed and domesticated forms appear. The cat and fox both have eyes that wax and wane with light, which may also suggest slyness or artifice. The wolf and dog are both genetically canine; the one wild, judged to be dirty and vicious, the other with its soft covering known for affection and companionship.[27]

From the autumn of 1993 until the summer of 1994 sisters had been dreaming, exploring, musing over the significance of images, opening their collective unconscious, talking to one another on new levels. Thus it was with Joseph's sisters that the step of theological reflection on dream themes took defined form and meaning.

The Chapter Event

All those who had participated over the eleven months were learning, opening themselves to a new perspective, listening within; moreover, they were doing the hard work of journalizing, discerning, and opening themselves to meaning. Levels of both expectancy and trepidation brought them to the Chapter meeting, the formal annual assembly of the Sisters of Saint Joseph of Nazareth, Michigan. The four "dream team" members who first suggested this venture had then been the ones who organized each step of the process, drawing well over one hundred and twenty women into their own enthusiastic world of collective dreaming. They reviewed for the 150 members of Chapter each step of the process, bringing forth skeptics who shared the surprises of their own personal dream discoveries. It was the skeptics who witnessed to their changed convictions regarding this very new approach to Chapter. Thus, the "dream team" prepared for theological reflection among the small groups.

There were twenty-one small groups, each with seven participants. Each person received a copy of the theme to be reflected on in her group. This theme statement included a summary drawn from all of the dream images touching on a common theme. It was important that this statement was limited to the sisters' understandings of its significance, and not the interpretations of the Program Director. On the reverse of the paper was a reference guide, quoting the pertinent sections of dreams touching on the theme. Each theme statement was accompanied by three questions to be considered from a faith perspective. A sample theme statement drawn from eighteen different dreams is entitled "Where We Have Positioned Ourselves as a Group: Sitting Back." It reads:

We have a long deep habit of taking an observer position (SSJ 21). We do not act on, or we turn our back on, opportunities (SSJ 29, 77) because we are more comfortable choosing the back seat where we can look to where the action is taking place "up front"(SSJ 62). We hesitate to speak up (SSJ 11) which causes us to stand off to the side (SSJ 53) or to take a back seat (SSJ 52, 54, 61, 62). We use time as an excuse to put off taking action (SSJ 50, 57, 58, 63, 70, 78). There are community gifts and talents, hidden under the guise of disability (SSJ 40) and pious interpretations of Joseph's humility (SSJ 54).[28]

Encouraging remedies for this "sitting back" stance occur in the images of a gate opening for us (SSJ 29). There is recognition that some of the membership have entered into engaging experiences(SSJ 39) and that it is time to move on (SSJ 37). The development of theme statements became a relevant instrument for the step of theological reflection.

In the use of theme statements, each sister was to bring a faith perspective to each of the themes her group considered. The first of the three theological reflection questions called for each sister to get in touch with her *own* experience of the theme in her personal life; for example, her own experience of "sitting back". The second question called for consideration of that theme experienced *as a congregation*, and ways in which each person felt that the community could grow in that particular area. The third question asked what this theme had to do with the business of Chapter, the specific practical issues which face any governing body. The reflection began with quiet shared silence. For ten minutes each sister sat in a circle of seven, reading the theme statement, getting in touch with her own feelings and experience. Then, round robin style, each sister shared with the others, and went on to reflect quietly on the collective expression of that theme. How does this theme exist among us? Is God calling us to a conversion here? How could we grow as a community of faith in this area? The third question inserted the whole project directly into the Chapter moment by inquiring: What, then, does this have to do with the practicalities of our life?

The allotted hour moved quickly with its alternating rhythms of quiet and vibrant exchange. Evidence that much was happening called for extending the sharing and discussion for an extra half an hour. The concluding responsibility of each group brought their reflection into focus as they formulated a Directional Statement. This statement, arising out of active engagement with the theme, responded to the need of the group to address the issue of their theme to the rest of the membership. The directional statement answered the question: What do we want to say to the membership of the Body, to ourselves, regarding *our* theme? All of the directional statements were collected and posted for the entire group to read. (The use of this type of statement would be further developed by the Ursuline Sisters of Bruno, as we shall see in the next chapter.) After a long break, the group was ready to celebrate.

Only another dream could satisfy the needs to summarize what Joseph's sisters were learning, to underline their cohesiveness, and to congratulate themselves for the completion of such a large endeavor. Even more, they needed to thank their God! Chapter Eight will describe how one hundred and fifty women—somewhat spontaneously—enacted, sang, danced, and laughed their way through a dream entitled Sing a New Song. The dream provided a rich and broad summary of the sisters' vocation and current place of spiritual growth and development. The fresh ritual of movement and song encompassed gestures of gratitude to their community leaders and concluded the project with tears of joy. Finally simple and profound commitment statements developed on the next day of Chapter reflected the effect of theological reflection on the sisters' life and place in the Church and became directives for the coming years.

CHAPTER THREE

Across a Continent: Awaking Ursuline Dreams

In the story of the community of Joseph's sisters we see the development of themes and theological reflection as clear advancement from the dream process of New Jerusalem. But my tracking of tribal dreams across the North American continent, begun as early as 1992, would provide an opportunity for directional statements to lead into powerful decision-making by 1996. It began after the year-long research in New Jerusalem, when I was ready for a lighter, fresher, perhaps quicker way to approach the tribal dream. The situation was to present itself in the Spring of 1992, as Ursuline nuns from across the North American continent were planning to converge in Cincinnati, Ohio. It was their first continental Ursuline Convocation. An invitation was made to present a workshop applying what I had learned about tribal dreams to a large group of religious communities. I filled out an application, submitting it with the title "Tribal Dreams," a term that attracted enough participants for two workshops. I knew that to present a viable and engaging event of tribal dreams to the Ursuline women who would be coming from Canada, the United States and Mexico, I would need to bring Ursuline samples of communal dreams. An Ursuline exploration of collective dreams called for Ursuline dreaming!

From my very first thoughts about collecting contemporary communal dreams, I felt instinctively that members of traditional, centuries-old communities, like Ursulines, would have a comfortable relationship with tribal dreams. "Groups, like individuals," wrote Carl Jung, "have a collective psyche and must differentiate in order to live their potential as fully as possible."[28] The emphasis of these dream ventures lies in appropriating the qualities attributed to the individual psyche and its dreams, and applying them to the dreams of intentional groups, like a support group, church community, or even one's poker club! Like the individual, a group develops an individuated collective psyche when its members have matured to the point that they can freely choose the community or leave it without loss of personal identity.

Dream work, therefore, can be carried out in any cohesive group as Henry Reed's experiment with a theoretical community would indicate.[30] During the United States bicentennial year, Reed collected dreams for the nation from his Sundance Community dreamers scattered across the nation. And others have experimented within short-term groups, like dream sharing groups. The Christian context is a natural one for such dreams because of Christianity's rich history both of symbol and of community.

Ursuline women, coming from a tradition begun in the early 1500's, are well acquainted with the life of the Spirit, which depends on dreams and images that arise in prayer and reflection. The sisters of my own congregation, the Ursuline Sisters of Brown County, Ohio, responded to a letter explaining my need to collect Ursuline dreams for the convocation. We agreed on June 19 as our common night of dreaming, marking from our community history of 1845 a date when our sisters had completed a long water journey from France to New York to Wheeling via ocean and canal, before proceeding to Cincinnati. The archetypal invitation which water offers as a symbol of birth, life and the depths of the unconscious, seemed to present an appropriate connection to this anniversary as we asked guidance for our present journey.

A wonderfully positive response allayed apprehensions that such a request would fall on cynical hearts—or at least skeptical ones. A certain amount of skepticism is no doubt helpful in raising questions, and these occurred with objective curiosity. There were understandable reservations among some. Our first Ursuline dream venture brought forth twenty-nine dreams with nineteen persons agreeing to come to discernment meetings, a time for exploring associations which the community could agree were authentic for us. For now, it is enough to say that fresh awareness is often the result of the reflection, dialog, and consensus that arise from the communal process of discernment. The first dream we encountered, <u>The Elusive Sprout</u>, spoke directly and simply to our reality.

The Elusive Sprout

I am on the back porch of the old main building at Brown County. I am struggling to get back into a pile some file-like secretarial folders and other "useless items" to return them to a shopping center. Said Center is situated very vaguely in the direction of Chatfield College.

A tiny green sprout keeps getting away from my pile. It is the only purchase that I wanted to keep - in hopes it would grow up next to the leaf-depleted section of my once beautiful umbrella plant (UBC, Spring,'92 - The Elusive Sprout, Bernadette B.).

What might be some meanings of this dream for our Ursuline congregation and its relationship to other dreams that had been submitted? We quickly noted images that seemed key to our communal story, like "the back porch." The back porch of the old main building, a motherhouse building now torn down, represents to us "what's behind us," an image of past religious life. The same building appears in another dream as that which we are escaping. "We," the membership of sisters, are making every effort to discover—as we see by the file-like secretarial folders and other "useless items"—a new organizing system. The old system of pre-Vatican II times no longer seems to work; moreover, paper files are made from trees no longer living. What was once helpful, is now useless.

Like most religious women we have been "shopping," often in life-giving secular places. Five dreams had shopping images in them! This could be considered negative or materialistic to some, but in another dream a group of women are walking "toward the village," like the shopping mall, *where the people are.* "Where the people are" appears also in the image of Chatfield College, as increasing numbers of our Appalachian adult neighbors are coming to receive educational opportunities unavailable to them before. This little college modeled some new directions for us. Two other dreams indicate that safety can be found in the direction of this place, where a century earlier (before refrigerators were available) an underground root cellar was the storage place for vegetables. Also presently located in this area is a large enclosed garden developed and tended by a sister well past ninety years. We agree that these two images point to the "roots" of our religious involvement with others as well as to the scriptural symbol of the spiritual life as an enclosed garden.

The tiny green sprout, a promising sign of new life, was one of numerous garden and plant images that appeared among our Ursuline dreams. This felt appropriate for a rural community but unexpected from women with chiefly urban backgrounds. The tiny fresh sprout is not to *replace* or uproot our "umbrella plant," but to take its own place next to it, presumably to flourish there. This plant is the only worthwhile purchase, reminding us of the merchant who, Matthew tells us, is searching for the finest pearl (Mt 13:45-46). It is true that the umbrella plant, our overall way of living, is no longer beautiful. It is depleted. We know that the "umbrella" refers to everything: our heritage, history, our future, and even our present—which, though less full numerically as in the past, is *not* dead. To be honest, the overall is depleted, but then, what contemporary traditional community has not suffered diminishment? This short dream with its back porch, secretarial folders, shopping center, Chatfield College, tiny sprout, and umbrella plant gives us a ready description of our changing lives as Ursulines. All this appears in symbols which affirms our rural and urban settings as well as new ways of being in those places. The images of this little dream were repeated in various forms among other dreams. The dreams which originated in the Brown County Ursuline clan would be introduced at the North American Ursuline Convocation workshops as examples for interpretation and application by members representing some of the seventeen other Ursuline clans.

Struggling To be Born

Among the dreams of this collection there was one, submitted by Carolyn, a close associate of the community, in which an unknown "member" of the community appeared. Carolyn struggled with the image of a pregnant woman ready to give birth. Ready, but unwilling. "She concentrates on the discussion around her and hopes that if she can ignore the pains they will go away. . . . It is difficult to know that this woman is in labor; she is so controlled." Religious women, especially educators, have been taught to be in control; furthermore, the perfectionist ideal of earlier religious life would explain why they could scarcely be otherwise. Here was a revelation of the community Shadow that was uncomfortable to the point of humiliation. The "baby" is active in Carolyn's dream, begging the mother to cooperate, straining, "beating its fists against the wall, . . . gasping for air!" The vividly described panic of the baby in the birth process is colorful warning about our tendency to keep things at *status quo*, to lose consciousness of the life that has already been conceived, and to keep locked into the unconscious unknown or rejected parts of the communal soul (UBC31). At this point in time the community was in denial about the obvious new life attempting to come forth, to be born.

The unrecognized Shadow appears again when Mary Eugenia's dream indicates that "I" am leaving the hospital, leaving behind some of my "illness." She finds that her car is blocked by shining white stones, and she (we) must progress by going backwards (UBC26). There is a sense that we must back off from the "shining white stones" of our idealism; moreover, the image of progressing backwards has historic connotations for this Ursuline community. Recent new historical investigations have put the membership in connection with core values of their past, the original 1535 foundation and lifestyle. The sisters have entered deeply into the writings of Angela Merici, the woman who first gathered those who were to be known as The Company of Saint Ursula.

A more encouraging relationship between the Shadow and the developing communal individuation arises in Chrissie P.'s description of her dream trek in green and white gym shoes. *Traveling on foot to a social justice meeting, she comes*

38

upon a hill, covered with snow. Pulling herself sideways up the hill, grasping bushes and tree limbs, finally out of breath at the top, she discovers that not only are "my clothes and shoes untouched, . . . [but] all the bushes and leaves on the trees are in full bloom" (UBC Dream 071992, <u>Moving Into God's Eye</u>, Chrissie P.). So, in spite of our challenges and strained efforts, there are discoveries of protection and growth which delight us. Here, as in the first dream experiment, the "I" of the dreamers has become identified with the "we" of the group.

The "I" of an individual dream refers to the ego-conscious dimension of the person which is recognized as that person visible and acting in the external reality. For one's self it is the person I recognize myself to be, deciding to get up in the morning, go to work, or *not* to get up and take action in my life. Sometimes, the ego-conscious part of the individual is simply an observer in the dream. Often, it is active, engaged, or undergoes a transformation in the dream. When the ego-conscious, or ego-aware self is applied to the *communal* dream, however, dreamers have recognized the identified *membership body* of the group or community. These are the acting, deciding persons who make up the group, named and visible as such. The membership, then, in a tribal dream is represented in its identified form as the "ego" of the community.

In the image cited above, therefore, Carolyn represents the community watching itself in the birth process but unable to assist. Our experience of "progressing backward" recalls the essential meaning of our foundational history, as well as our need to "back off" some of our idealism. Chrissie is "us" as we take the uphill struggle toward social justice, discovering the blooming beauty amidst the cold of winter snow. Without these signals from within the unconscious of the community members, they may never detect unrecognized arenas of their inner world.

A final reference quotes yet another of the twenty-nine dreams received by the Ursulines of Brown County. Here the fullness of life in the community is revealed in a dream of wisdom figures. Here the Shadow makes its appearance in its unknown, often surprising beauty. The dreamer finds herself laughing and talking amidst a group of elderly sisters:

> *Suddenly each one of them begins to change, . . . becoming younger and younger. Finally the process stops when each one reaches the age when she entered the convent. They are fresh and young and lovely. In their faces there is a look of joyful anticipation; they are full of enthusiasm to give themselves to the Lord. Deeply touched, I begin to weep and someone asks: 'Why are you crying?' I answer, 'Because you are all so beautiful.' Everyone laughs happily* (UBC Dream, 071992 - <u>The Young and the Beautiful</u>, Marjean C.).

Dreams for an Alternative Way of Life

As tribes will do, Ursulines are made up of smaller clans who gather to collaborate on issues of lifestyle, social justice, education of new members, and global concerns. Nine of these clans, autonomous in themselves but with long historical connections, form a group called the Ursuline Society. Scattered across the Midwest of the United States, both their leadership councils and grassroots members meet occasionally during the year. Within the leadership, various committees have arisen to define collaboration and joint action in defined areas. One such committee is the Way of Life committee.

The Way of Life committee was originally composed of six women from three clans. Within the Ursuline Society they represent nuanced differences in location, size, degree of institutional framework, and forms of governance. All are living in the throes of current transitions arising from global changes and shifting patterns within the lives of sisters in the Catholic Church. It is their purpose to explore on an experiential level what it would look like to live incorporating the spiritual and religious values of the 1535 founding Company into contemporary living. In other words, what does it mean to live as Angela Merici, the foundress, lived?

The participants decided to seek a description of that life by opening their unconscious to the possibilities. Mandala drawing and dreaming were employed as the means of doing this. The collected images described the truth of their current situation as Ursulines and as religious women, even while pointing out their direction and affirming their future. In the mandala work, an umbilical cord appeared in one of the pieces. As all entered into association with images of the dreams, the umbilical cord again appeared.

> *I am on a downhill road. I am holding a <u>cord</u> as I ease the rolling car down the hill. As I look down a side street toward a parallel street on the right where another car has crashed, I am intensely focused, exerting myself strongly to maintain the car rolling, not crashing* (WOL Dream, 021495 - <u>Rolling, Not Crashing</u>, Cabrini D.).

Cabrini's dream shows us where we are "on the downhill road" of religious life. We are "holding the cord as we ease the rolling car down the hill." We know that some aspects of our life must "go downhill," but as we exert ourselves we are holding tightly to the source of life and nourishment. Mary Ellen, another Way of Life member, dreamed that we "see [our] own face. The left side . . . is peeling away in layers. It is scary" (WOL2). Our feminine side, long covered by the masculine law and character of the Catholic Church, is finally being revealed—and it's scary. In yet another dream we are all in a king-sized bed together, revealing a desire to be incorporated into the "family." In this family the "mother" is very ill, yet gets out of bed to offer [us] food (WOL3). Finally, "we" are standing at the familiar fork of two Cincinnati streets. On one side the traffic runs smoothly to a shopping area in a somewhat affluent neighborhood; on the other, the less convenient, heavily trafficked side, the street moves past the Veterans' Hospital, past the zoo, through a poor residential neighborhood. There are extensive hospital facilities to the right of this whole area, and a university complex on the left (WOL5).

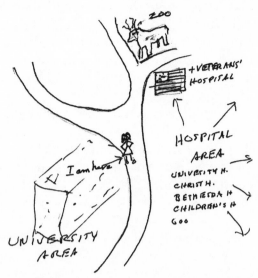

As tribal or collective dreams, these images address Ursuline life and the purpose of the WOL Committee. A common theme is that of a quest: how do we keep life "rolling without crashing?" What is happening to the group's identity? How do we incorporate "this woman" into the family of the Church? And, at this critical juncture, which road do we take—the easier, more comfortable one or the older, instinctual path, the Gospel path which always leads to life among the poor and broken?

The Ursuline Society Listens to Its Tribal Dreams

The Ursuline dream experience among the Ursulines of Brown County, Ohio, had filtered into the Way of Life Committee, representing six communities of Ohio, Kentucky and Illinois. It was the desire of the members of the Way of Life committee to extend their experience of communal dreaming to include the wider Ursuline Society leadership scattered across the mid-West. A recurring movement *into* our dreams and *out to* action had been chosen as central to our procedure. So when a synchronistic invitation to the annual meeting arrived with the following inclusion, it resonated with our feelings: "It is clear from her writings and the research on her life that Angela was a strong, independent spiritual woman. Her life was one of an *inward-outward* movement. . . . It was decided to place the entire context and content (of our gathering) within the framework of the inward-outward movement as it applies to Ursuline women which, in turn, overflows into our ministry with [others]" (Letter from the Ursuline Society Steering Committee).

In spite of a long agenda of necessary business, the Way of Life committee immediately requested time on that agenda. Those coming together had once developed a limited history of networking and collaboration, then later had joined together to strengthen and extend their bonds. Governmentally independent of one another, they had proceeded under the concerted leadership of their separate governing bodies to collaborate on increasing levels, particularly in the areas of Angela Merici's spirituality and their 450 years of shared ancestry. Every meeting seemed filled with necessary agenda items; however, this one presented the risk of bringing our personal inner dream movement to the outer discernment of the gathered "clans."

As the meeting convened with an evening session, the WOL group invited those present into their experience. It was explained that it had happened quite spontaneously among them at a difficult juncture in their work, a time when they had reached such a point of weariness that an impasse had been created. At that moment they had agreed to surrender to the Spirit, Who always seemed to arise among them at vulnerable times, and to ask for some message or guidance by way of dreams.

Now the committee asked from the Society a bit of blind trust! Explaining that in this opening session they were not interested in long academic explanations of whether, how, or why God may communicate in dreams, they invited those present to join them in accepting certain defined assumptions:

1. Based on the Judeo-Christian scriptures, God speaks to the beloved in sleep;
2. The message of God for the community comes through dreams to individuals;
3. Symbol has been affirmed in the Catholic tradition of sacraments and ritual as a source of breakthrough to grace;
4. If tribal dreams have continued to be accepted by primitive peoples, to be directive for them, then as humans and as Christians we can expect that *our* tribal dreams are available to us;
5. Carl Jung's theorizing on the collective psyche was based on long term study of cultures throughout the world;
6. Henry Reed, a more contemporary researcher, backed up these reflections of Jung in his Community Sundance explorations of the late 1970's and early 1980's;
7. A dream is a total description of the communal soul, a three-dimensional one. As Jeremy Taylor emphasizes in his writings, every layer of one's life experience is present in the dream: state of health, work life, primary relationships. Surely the communal layer is a key aspect of our lives.

In conclusion, the group was assured that the nature of their intentionality would serve to highlight the communal nature of their personal dreams.

Under the pressure of time, the process was reduced to great simplicity: "Turn to God, open your soul to God's word; ask for a dream; give focus by some simple gesture, movement and/or prayer. Do not be concerned that all members may not remember a dream." Experience has shown that usually about one-fourth of those participating have no dream to bring to the discernment process. This is not to presume, however, that their lack of a dream does not affect the soul of the group and in this way strengthen the overall experience. Tentatively for some, there was, nevertheless, an expectant hope among the group for insights and feelings into the communal soul of the entire Ursuline Society.

Tentativeness and doubt shifted to playful acceptance the next morning as an abundance of dreams descended upon the session. A crossover effect appeared as the group identified repeated images in different persons' dreams. Twelve themes re-occurred, including: journey with a sense of direction, communication, a sense of largeness, and the influence of the masculine principle. Beyond this was a collection of unique images, that is, events, feelings, or persons that appeared only once in the dreams, but were so cogent in their Ursuline implications as to grip the group with clarity and excitement. The resulting work was an example of a group risking to bring their personal inner movement of a dream to the outer discernment of the gathered "clans." One of the participants in the Ursuline Society dream exploration recognized a possible solution to a vexing problem facing her own Bruno, Saskatchewan congregation.

The Ursulines of Bruno Discern Their Future Options

> I am back in our old one-room school. On one side stands a tall cabinet where the "radio/ gramophone," is kept. I open the doors of the cabinet and see that the inside leads into rooms which I had never known to have been there when I was a kid! Ana, our Brazilian and youngest member of our community is with me, together with other young people. . . . We walk from one room to another putting on the lights. . . .
>
> In the kitchen, on a huge stove, are a number of pots and pans, covered with a big cloth which in turn is covered with dust as though it hasn't been touched for a long time. The rooms are all of this nature as if no one had passed through here for a long time.
>
> In one of the central rooms there is an opening in the ceiling which seems to be an opening into a steeple....There is a ladder leading to the opening. . . .
>
> As we start to leave I put out the lights, but can't manage to put them all out. I can't understand why not, because I use the same switches as I had for putting them on. When I shut one off, another goes on (BRU 1, 112596 - Keeping the Lights On, Claire N.).

Here is an image of the first school which the sisters from Bruno, Saskatchewan, opened on the prairies of Canada. This is one of the "pioneer spirit" dreams which the sisters immediately related not only to their first missions, but to the unapologetic sense of themselves as "prairie chickens," and also to themselves as those who have weathered many difficulties.

Earlier, Bernadine, one of these Bruno sisters who had been present and involved in another dream enterprise, contacted me about the possibility of visiting her congregation in Bruno, Saskatchewan. Already the sisters had been engaged in a two-year process of discernment regarding their future. A small community of forty sisters, many of them aging, needed to continue the process—which at that time had reached no consensus—of a potential merger with a larger group. They planned to have a firm decision by the spring of 1998. After discussion of possible arrangements for facilitation of the group, Bernadine suggested to the membership that they enter as a group into a dream adventure.

Thus, their dream project began in the fall of 1996, to be concluded with a decision in the spring of 1998. November 25, the feast of Saint Catherine of Alexandria—a virgin-martyr greatly admired by Angela Merici and held in high esteem by the original Company—was chosen for an initial dream night. Preparation and plans were launched, and dreams recorded. The very first dream arrived from the sisters' Brazilian mission. Because of time constraints and the distances involved, our fax machines heated up. Within a year two meetings of the entire community were held. The first was a struggle with the objective data of the dream symbols, a time of association work, of interpretation—a "head" experience. The second meeting was to be "all heart." Of the forty members, all but the Brazilians and three persons in the infirmary were present, including two spiritually and intellectually savvy ninety-two year olds. The elderly women in the community brought the fruit of wisdom and their lifelong prayer to the interpretation of the symbols. Additional options, beyond the merger they were still considering, began to unfold and enthusiasm for these possibilities grew. Hope grew alongside, shaping a clearer sense of direction for their future.

Claire N.'s dream heralds reminders of the community's pioneer history, previewing basic elements that were to arise later in the discussions of the coming year. Key among these were eight symbols of the sisters' current situation, few of which had as yet been named. The meanings appeared in several repetitions.

The first element is the realization that more than one option was available for their future—"*I open the doors of the cabinet and see that the inside leads into rooms which I had never known to have been there when I was a kid!*" The word *opening* is reinforced by three repetitions.

The image of "*Ana, . . . with other young people*" indicates future promise of youth or new life, both in its third world diversity—"*Brazil*"—and in its reference to Ana as the youngest member of the community. Ana, herself, submitted a complete dream that extends this image of youth in the scriptural symbols of a garden.

"*Light,*" the third element, appears archetypally in almost all myth, legend and literature. Turning on lights assures us that we can see where we are and where we are going. It can be an assurance of insight or wisdom. "We," the membership, are now walking from one space to another, looking over the situation. However, having accomplished this, "we" find that now "*[We] can't manage to put them all [the*

44

lights] out. [We] can't understand why not, . . . When we shut one off, another goes on."
It is almost amusing how the dreamer makes efforts to shut off the lights; however, once having received an understanding, having seen the meaning in a situation, it is impossible *not* to have the insight, even if one does not wish to follow its implications.

Just turning on the lights launches the beginning of a transformation, symbolized by the *"kitchen,"* the fourth element, where raw material is transformed into edible nourishment. The resources of the kitchen are present but have not been used, and have been allowed to grow *"old, and dusty."* The *"radio/gramophone,"* the old manner of communication, seems no longer to be available. The *"old, one room school"* has given way to wider, more varied spaces. The *"huge stove [with its] pots and pans,"* the basic source of energy and the equipment for carrying out the transformation, have been covered over. Note that most of these resources have not been lost or destroyed, just overlooked for some time. These symbols hint to the communal membership that they need to get in touch with their oldest and most fundamental resources which are present and waiting.

The *"central room,"* the sixth element, logically follows awareness of fundamental resources. The "center" in psychology and in spirituality points the individual or group to the core self, where all is whole, where all is at peace. It appears in the writings of the great Saint Teresa of Avila as the center of the interior castle. Centering practices such as yoga, Tai Chi, Qigong, or centering prayer, serve to lead their practitioners to the nonnegotiable inner truth of the Self. In Christian understanding, it is the place where God dwells within each person, the place within the most evil of persons that still remains an unviolated place of innocence.

Right in this center, the biggest hint of all appears in the form of a ladder leading upward, in a heavenly direction. Again notice that the word *opening* is repeated three times as if there were triple dream exclamation points: *"opening in the ceiling, opening to a steeple, ladder into the opening."* The significance of this symbol is related in Ursuline history to the mystical experience of Angela Merici. It was as a young peasant girl that Angela's future was revealed in the image of the ladder between heaven and earth. The ladder was filled with joyous pairs of maidens singing, accompanied by pairs of angels playing musical instruments. The vision set the direction for Angela's life work, a Company which defied the politics and customs of the time by offering liberating choices to women. There was an "opening," a way out of the dilemma: an unsuitable arranged marriage or enclosed monastic life. Angela was offered both and said that she chose the third option. She chose a life of virginal service, centered in relationship with Christ and characterized by contemplative joy.

The unwilling lights were, of course, a sign of hope: "When I shut one off, another goes on!" This image was to provide a humorous conclusion to the sisters' coming decision. The dream provided all that was needed by these pioneer women to celebrate the conclusion of their long discernment about choosing a future. The entire process had continued for over four years. In the latter part of this time, the

45

dreams had focused their movement, and through profound research, dialogue, and theological reflection, had brought them 180° from their original 1994 direction.

Directional Statements

In the last chapter, reading the story of the Sisters of Saint Joseph of Nazareth, we saw the arrival of a new approach that used directional statements to facilitate the process of Chapter work. This approach, not included in the original New Jerusalem project, has developed over several experiments. It blossomed for the Bruno sisters into an important turning point in their decision about their future.

Directional statements are formulated by small groups and directed to their larger membership. How the other members apply them is an important aspect of moving the dream work into realistic decision or action. For the Bruno Ursulines, as they were drawing upon the riches of their collective unconscious in order to reach a decision about their future existence as a community, the fifteen directional statements moved them forward in very specific ways. The directional statements outlined the final actions to be taken leading to the decision, and, perhaps as crucially, the directives described those core values which became the *criteria* for the decision-making itself. These steps would affect their future viability as a community and as a people on mission. Fourteen specific action directives culminated in the last statement, naming the astounding criteria for decision-making in the following terms:

> IN APRIL OF 1998, THE BRUNO URSULINE COMMUNITY WILL
> APPROACH THEIR FUTURE IN (THIS) PIONEERING SPIRIT:
>   LETTING GO OF THE OPTIONS THAT OFFER SECURITY AND
>   COMFORT,
>   LIMITING OURSELVES TO THOSE OPTIONS THAT CALL US TO
>   FAITH, COURAGE, TRUST IN GOD,
>   RISKING THE NEW, AND
>   SERVING THE COMMON GOOD.

These criteria, rooted in the gospels, paved the way for deciding the future of a community.

The Flowering of the Pioneering Spirit

And decide they did! It had been literally eight years since the Bruno sisters first began to reflect seriously on the possibilities that their community might dissolve, merge with another larger group, or move in yet a different direction than either of these options. Now, in three days of profound personal and communal prayer, these women moved seamlessly through the process of discerning which of the five options before them would create their future. In large and small groups they faced one another with honesty and love, wrestled with the values and issues they had brought to the surface during a year and a half of research, then decided. They chose the broadest option, the one which best represented the criteria they had set. They chose to "Risk Something New!" They defined this in terms of selling their large, empty motherhouse, a place of myth, history and tradition that roots them in the past. They knew it was time to let go; furthermore, they declared their intention to move their central house to a new location and to take a corporate stance on a value that would identify them as a group.

What of the four options not chosen? The Chapter body identified values within each of these which remained non-negotiable, and which they intended to build into their choice of a renewed pioneer spirit. Strongest of these values was the development of strong relationships and opportunities for collaboration with other prairie Ursuline groups. The prairie mindset of Western Canada, as described by independent research, is willing to risk, is entrepreneurial, and is as open as the great skies of the prairies. The hard work of deciding accomplished, a birthday party concluded this "futures" aspect of the Chapter.

When the time for celebration finally arrived, five birthday cakes with glowing candles were brought into the Chapter room. Sister Ursula, one of the oldest wise women present, offered a cake one by one to each of the four research groups whose option was *not* chosen. In each case the Chapter chanted, "We had hoped that this option would provide a new birth for our community. Now, O God, we release this option to you." Then the candles on that cake were blown out. When they came to the cake representing their choice for the future, the sisters sang a lusty Happy Birthday to themselves. One of the research group stepped forward and blew. The lights on the candles wavered, shrank, then burst back into full flame. Others came forward to assist. A giant blast of effort. Again, the candle flames flickered wildly, and again burst into flame. It wasn't hard to "get the message," and by now the group was laughing as the candles refused to be snuffed out. Claire N., who could not turn off the lights of the pioneer school, then reread her dream with tears of understanding that "the promise made [them] by the Lord would be fulfilled" (Luke 1:45). Their lights were not destined to be easily turned off.

The next morning the sisters would take the confirming step of beginning the process to elect the persons who would best lead them into their chosen future. A fresh dream then appeared.

>   I am walking alone outside between the trees when I hear someone call for help. I run and there is Marian, very pregnant and ready to give birth. I am very worried about what the people will think seeing a sister pregnant. I tell her I'd go for help because I haven't any experience as a midwife.
>   I run to the convent, worried because I am leaving her alone. I say to the sisters, "Run, Marian's going to have a baby <u>now</u>." Some of these run, and I run ahead and let her rest her head on my lap. Every other sister who arrives has

something in her hands to help. We all make a circle around her. Marian laughs and cries at the same time. I wipe her face with a cloth and say, "Don't be afraid. I was born in the same way." Another sister says, "Open your legs because <u>the birth is happening now</u>." I say that I think we need the help of a midwife because none of us has had the experience.

Someone goes to call one. I don't go because I don't want to miss what is happening. When the midwife arrives, she looks just like Marian. I ask, "Marian, do you have a sister who looks like you?" She just smiles and the midwife helps cut the umbilical cord. Sister Claudia helps to wash the baby (who is very messy) and everyone wants to see and hold it.

It really is a big celebration. Some laugh and some cry because they feel it deeply (BRU 041898 - <u>Pregnant With Life</u>, Ana Lucia D.].

Having decided for a wide open future, the sisters were now ready to choose new leadership. Again the criteria were clear. "In light of our call to a Family Spirituality; in light of contemporary developments in religious life, in the Church, and in the culture; and of our stated expectations of leadership, WHO ARE THE PERSONS WHO CAN BEST LEAD US TO THE FUTURE WE HAVE CHOSEN?" Indeed, Sister Marian was chosen as leader of the community with three councilors to form the leadership team.

Coming as it did, after three days of "labor," but before the elections, the dream above was introduced with excitement to a few at breakfast on the morning of elections. Ana Lucia was deeply excited by the feelings of the dream. At that point we saw the image of Marian as representing all the leadership of the community. The community, by its decision for the future, is at this time giving birth. It is cutting the umbilical cord to the past by putting its motherhouse up for sale. Ana Lucia, "born in the same way," had been born in her Brazilian home with the assistance of a midwife. The "open legs," indicate birth, but also perhaps the readiness to take the next step. Everyone is a part of the birth, doing her part in research, dialogue, sharing, and prayer. Sister Claudia, a motherly sister who has a high value for tradition and law, is there to remind the community that the birth will need to have some structure to provide for cleaning up the mess that births—and transitions—inevitably produce. The journey of courage taken by these mediumistic women provides a model for others to trust the gift of the dreams, which rises unceasingly from within the communal soul.

CHAPTER FOUR

A Family's Dreams Reveal Its Transformation

I am in a big, OLD house....lots of rooms. I am fascinated by this house because I love old things. I sense that (it) holds something very special for me....I will find a treasure here. I can't wait to explore. All the rooms in the house are filled with crafts because a holiday craft fair is being held here...The atmosphere is festive and relaxed. I am with my mom and my sister. I know that the house will belong to me when the craft show is over so, although I am excited about exploring it, I am very O.K. with the fair and all these people being here (who are milling around).

I move to a room and notice that the wall is covered with wallpaper. But instead of the wallpaper being glued to the wall, it is hanging from a wooden dowel rod. I go over to get a closer look. As I pull the wallpaper toward me, I see that there are <u>many</u> layers of paper beneath the outermost layer. The top layer of paper is unremarkable; nothing special or spectacular. All of the subsequent layers are Christmas wrapping paper and there are approximately 20 layers. I continue to leaf through all the layers. I am surprised that the layers are Christmas paper. I am trying to get to the bottom of all of them.

When I finally reach under the last piece of paper, I see and touch a plastered, rough wall. The rough textured portion of the wall separates the old, heavy, rough hewn log beams that the house is made of. It looks like the wall of an old log cabin home. I feel surprised. I expected something different—more fancy. But then I feel that, no, this is the way it SHOULD be; this is RIGHT.

I sense that this is the treasure I was to find. My house is an authentic, original, REAL log cabin. And it's mine!! I am so excited! (BOS 19, 110897 - Beneath the Wallpaper, Marianne B.)

Introduction to the Family

It is a crisply cold Sunday morning as I negotiate the labyrinthine suburban streets. There are neither big old houses with lots of rooms nor log cabins in sight. The dream above becomes the matrix of the dream process about to begin, hinting at an archetypal birth that is happening, multi-layered as it is. Brunch is waiting at the Bosch family home, and I am feeling expectant and hopeful, although only one of the seven family members feels very sure about the adventure we are about to undertake together.

From the beginning it is clear that the family process will be somewhat different than that of larger groups. How different? I am not sure, but feel it will make itself known organically along with our need to understand the dreams. The size of the group is the first and most obvious difference. It lends itself to both informality and a manageable number of dreams. It also triggers personal response to individual patterns of growth and experience that may blur the description of the *family* psyche. The manner of working must unfold one step at a time, each one designed from the results of the one before.

Marianne, the wife and mother of the family, has brought to her family the dream seminar discoveries about new ways to meet God and to pray. Her enthusiasm and the good sportsmanship of her husband and children have opened the way for me to present the possibilities of tribal dreaming. Instinctively I know that this will be a different experience than that of the larger groups. John, husband and father, a pharmacist, is a committed Catholic who, like his wife and children, is willing to hear what it might mean for the family to listen to God through their dreams. None of us is certain where we will be led from there.

After a brief brunch, we continue to sit at the dining room table and review the material which I have brought for each one. There is some nervous laughter and shifting, some teasing exchanges, as we begin; yet, the festive air of the dream is evident as we begin to explore "the big, old house of this family." Lori, a flight attendant, is already living outside their home; Joe, next in line, studies at a nearby university in the ROTC Air Force program. Johnny, a junior at a local Catholic high school, is involved with service in their home parish. Tess, at thirteen, has reservations about what the expectations of the dream project might be and whether she can live up to them. David, the 12 year old, jumps in with shy but focused questions.

As the dream material grounds our conversation, the group focuses on what this plan might mean. The ordinary concerns of new dreamers about remembering, recording, and making sense arise. Agreement is made to use the next three weeks for dreaming, rather than to choose one night. I give each one a self-addressed envelope for mailing me the dreams directly; another option is to give them to Marianne, who sees me weekly as reader, typist and secretary.

The Family Process Begins

The dreams pour in! Twenty-five before the three weeks are over. Marianne and I review the dreams and the comments which each person has added to his or her dream story. We supplement with our own suggestions for possible meanings, prepare copies of everything, and send them to each member to read before the second Sunday brunch. At this second session we are to begin the somewhat arduous work of association and reflection on the images as revelatory of the family life. At this point the family sees itself as "unremarkable, nothing special or spectacular."

Our second gathering occurs in late November, another cold and sunny autumn day. The task is to bring to the surface those qualities of each family member which carry some aspect of family energy. All of them appear in one another's dreams, expressing some characteristics of the family. They begin to "peel back" some of the family layers, beginning gingerly, though respectfully.

Dad, 45, and Mom, 44, are described by the five children in archetypal terms. Dad—he was informed by his children's awareness of him—is the provider. He is a worker, quiet, gentle but firm. A sensitive man with one possible exception. At various sports events, Dad "urges us on," Joe says. "He's obnoxious," David adds with a certain simplicity. Looking a bit pained, John indicates that he sees himself as a motivator, an observation which both the formal and informal moments of the dream gatherings seemed to support. John is the public face of the family, aware in one dream that he is expected to be a "model" to his sons, but in ways which are not always comfortable (BOS16). In one of David's dreams John corrects him, in another, pubescent David now sits in his father's big blue chair.

Mom is always available to them, the "large woman" in one of Lori's dreams. The family experiences her as passionate, enthusiastic, outspoken about her convictions, even quick-tempered in this regard. Mom is a "go-getter," they say about their middle-aged Mom. Mom is also the worrier. She runs her home with great warmth, and is engaged in training for Church ministry. It is she who had signed up for the dream seminar that was later to become so important for the family's view of themselves. Marianne's dreams are constant discoveries of the basic beauties and values of life, of new ventures, and of inner wisdom. In her relatively frequent appearances in the family dreams, "Mom" is present in the home as one who sets values, who nourishes, who "cleans up." She is concerned for each one, and as one dream describes her, is blind to everything but the good qualities in her family. She is blind to all that may be ugly in them.

Lori is described as the family member who has most changed and grown. She is someone to whom the others look up. It is Lori who has faced up to poor decisions made at a younger age, and taken responsibility for them. She is trustworthy, the family agrees, yet a fun-lover. Compassionate, yet critical and judgmental, Johnny says that Lori is a leader. Lori's dreams are filled with her search for identity as an adult, rejecting her image as a "dumb blonde." When she comes into the others' dreams, she is companion or one to be protected from danger. It is the change in Lori that has shaped the family transformation about to be discovered.

Joe, 19, is quickly identified as carrying the jokester aspect of the family soul. "He is an instigator," Tess injects and all agree as Joe grins approvingly. Joe, a busy ROTC member at a local university, is also open-minded, compassionate and in touch with his feelings. Joe, as others in the family have been, is at ease naming qualities where he recognizes a need for change. He admits his impatience and low tolerance for disorder. Joe's dreams deal with the power and powerlessness of masculine energy, and the beauty of the feminine. The others' dreams find him strong, resourceful, and someone who leads in frightening times.

Johnny, 15, a self-proclaimed perfectionist, is described as a person of stick-to-itiveness. Although open-minded about many things, he tends to be the family hermit, keeping to himself. Perhaps this relates to the family's description of him as being a deeply emotional and sensitive person, yet capable of sarcasm. The arts and poetry are important to him. Excitement and tension permeate his dreams with their repeated images of oppositeness and "two's." His dream, Who Nose, tells us that his "nose" only *hurts* when it "lines up perfectly down the middle of my face" (BOS8).

Tess, 13, is the teaser! She "knows what buttons to push." Tess is thoughtful and insightful, bringing a healthy level of questioning and skepticism to the dream process. She is, however, dependent and vulnerable, acknowledging that it is the little things that "get to her." Mom says that Tess has jumped into adolescence with both feet. Her "Shadow" dream indicates that she knows already that life is not always OK. On the other hand, her own image of the family as a car appeals to the rest of the family as an image of constant movement and change, but "never being on the highway alone." Tess enters David's dreams as sister, friend and companion, someone with him on life's adventures.

Finally, the family's spontaneous response to David, 12, is to give him the persona of the family athlete. David is easy-going and a potential leader, always aware of others. He is also artistic and affectionate. Being very lovable assures that he usually gets his own way. David, like Johnny, admits to a strong sense of perfectionism. From the time the dream process begins, David's dream life "takes off." He continues to pursue the dream images and their message about transition into adolescence. Filled with questions for which he does not yet have answers, David's dreams are clearly puberty dreams. In one dream he is "looking toward the Griffins' house." A little research indicates a medieval griffin as a half-eagle, half-lion creature. Is David—and his family—ready to soar and to roar?

A pattern the members of the family begin to hear among themselves is their need to "do it right," to be the image of the perfect family, and to become irritated with themselves when they fail to meet this expectation. Perfectionism seems more imbedded in high Catholic ideals than in competition among themselves, although that latter quality appears in other individual activities outside the household. This perfectionism may, indeed, be the plaster that both remains rough and holds the strength of their truest inner identity.

Having named, in that second gathering, the way in which each separate member carried traits or characteristics of the whole family, one dream is introduced from each member of the family, using it to associate with the images and feelings which relate to the family psyche. Everyone interacts enthusiastically.

The dream experiment itself appears in the dream themes as a source of transformation. There is a sense of fun, so the two and half hours with one break covers a lot of territory. Dream work follows excited chatter. The group seems energized by the project as a heightened awareness deepens their sense of identity as family. The time concludes with an invitation for them to continue in pairs or small groups, each tracing patterns or images through all the dreams. John and David work on three major themes that have appeared: the themes of opposites, of the masculine, and of animals. Marianne and Joe move through the dreams to identify transformation images, houses/rooms, and body images. Lori, Johnny and Tess seek out the patterns of feelings, of Shadow, and of the feminine.

A third meeting follows many weeks of my sifting through the dreams. More dreams have been submitted, especially by Lori and David. As facilitator, my instincts finally begin to sense what is happening and to recognize the current family "moment." I have spent eight to ten hours with them, have watched the happy interplay, have enjoyed the loving teases, and experienced the camaraderie among them. I have entered deeply into reflection on their dreams and their responses to them. Is this family too good to be true? Perfectionists, are they always putting their best foot forward for the visiting dream facilitator?

The opening meeting had seemed to say otherwise. John had commented then that in a former family counseling situation they were not able to share openly with one another; but in this situation everyone had shared in openness and trust. Marianne questions whether they have yet reached such a place, but "are moving toward it. Desiring it! Change is at once alluring and repellent. It's exciting but scary." She continues prophetically, "I think we are a family on the verge of a new birth," not realizing that the Christmas wallpaper of her Beneath the Wallpaper dream is already pointing to a celebration of a birth, revealing the most authentic description of their collective psyche.

Each has entered into naming one another's gifts and quirks with honesty, yet reverence. But, recognizing and naming the Shadow is still a tender area. At the second meeting Lori has referred obliquely to an undefined adolescent crisis. Thus the primeval and inevitable pattern of death and life begins to reveal itself. What has emerged is that this "too perfect" family is actually on the positive side of a family transformation. They have moved from the critical experience of Lori's two adolescent pregnancies to a place of being a joyous blended family with overlays of transition occurring in all of their lives.

Lori's Story

My mother shows up at my home for a surprise visit. Only she is a very large woman who doesn't resemble my mom at all - and she's blind. I have dark hair.

There is an ugly chair in my living room that was Mom's chair. I try to help her to it but she needs no help. It's as if she's drawn to it. She sits down and exclaims, "Oh, my chair." Then she says that it must have shrunk. I tell her that the chair is ugly. It doesn't look good in my living room. "It only looks good with you in it, Mom." The chair's fabric is of many bright colors.

The rest of the living room is drab. There is no decorative scheme to it. . . . The rest of the furniture is just blurs. Suddenly I realize that it is not the chair that is ugly, it is the entire room. I need to decorate my living room. My mother says, "Throw it out!" What an odd statement. I assume she means to start from scratch (BOS 5, 102697 - The Ugly Chair, Lori B.).

When an adolescent pregnancy occurs in such a "perfect" Catholic family, *the* issue must arise! What will the neighbors think? What will our friends at Church say? Marianne finds in herself an attitude of defensiveness. She is ready to fight for her daughter and her family. And what of her own mother and sisters, and the rest of the family? Marianne's mother warns her not to tell "grandma" because it might cause her to have a stroke. The perfectionism which the family named at their very first dream project meeting is with them as a permanent member of the family! At this point Marianne confronts the "yellow dog" of Bosch Dream 7. She finds her voice and decides to *tell* grandma. Grandma listens, commiserates, and supports, as have her two sisters. As Marianne pulls back the layers of the family identity, to her relief, she receives only compassion and understanding from her friends and associates at Church.

Lori relates, "My freshman year in high school is when I lost my best friend. I started hanging out with other people. Shortly after is when the eating disorder set in. [Looking for a school with a more person-oriented approach], I transferred to a different school, recovering slowly from the anorexia." Marianne recalls from Lori's early childhood, how friends and strangers alike made frequent and public comments about her beauty. As any mother, Marianne worried about the effect of this on the other children; now however, she wonders about the relationship of these repeated experiences on Lori's sense of self-image. Lori had already been getting counseling for anorexia during her sophomore year, and by the summer between her sophomore and junior years, she felt really good about herself. That summer she began to eat normally. "I'd like to say I am recovered from the eating disorder," Lori says. "The food thing doesn't bother me anymore. I eat normally but an eating disorder is about more than food. I still think that feeling out of place and needing to be perfect still affects me."

Lori continues, "The summer between my sophomore and junior year I met a large group of people at the swim club and we became really close. Then when the school year came around we all went our separate ways. I had transferred schools again. One of the guys I hung around with was also going there but I didn't have any girlfriends. I really didn't have the support of other girls my age." Lori started dating a guy of whom others disapproved. He was her first serious boyfriend who, although he attended AA meetings, drank a lot. John and Marianne's deep disapproval only gave Lori more reason to continue the relationship. He paid attention to her, but looking back, she realizes that "he just used me to drive him around since he didn't have a car. At this point I'd say he was a loser." After they broke up, Lori began dating another young man who shared some of her classes and consoled her when the other relationship faltered. But "my relationship with 'Alan' went one step too far. I had some girlfriends then but no one close. I felt then, and still do today, when I come into an already established group, like I'm the outsider. Other girls grew up together, had gone to school together and 'Alan' was more genuine and cared for me."

Lori was sixteen when she became pregnant. When she told Alan, he said he would support her no matter what she decided to do. Although he didn't turn against her, Lori now realizes that "I made it seem like he did. I was angry with myself and it made it easier to blame someone else. I prayed every night that I would wake up in the morning and be on my period and it would all be a bad nightmare." She remembers her mother found a note in her wastebasket about birth control pills. In discussing pregnancy Marianne told Lori that she must take responsibility for her actions, "so the whole time I knew I was pregnant that thought was running through my head. I knew I was too young to leave home. At that point, the only other option I knew of was abortion. Alan and I went to an abortion clinic. As soon as we stepped into it, I knew this wasn't right. I knew this was not the answer."

Lori was six months pregnant when her parents found out. Marianne knew Lori was gaining weight but, fearing the anorexia, hesitated to say anything about a weight gain; soon, however, the school guidance counselor called Marianne to tell her that she had reason to suspect that Lori was pregnant. "My mom and dad BOTH came up in my room that day," Lori recounted. "I knew they knew because my dad never came in my room let alone with my mom. I was scared but it was a relief to tell someone, especially my parents, because my mom and dad are always there for me." Lori recognized her parents' disappointment and anger. They were worried because she hadn't seen a doctor, and thus had no way of knowing the baby's health, or Lori's. But from that point on Lori felt that things were better.

At school, things went on as usual. Many girls were in the same situation as Lori. When people at school found out that Lori was considering open adoption, she was put in touch with another girl who'd done this the year before. Sharing this young woman's story brought some relief and help. The idea of open adoption had come up almost immediately. Lori knew she couldn't mother this baby, and this sounded like a good alternative.

Marianne and John had met a couple who were trying to adopt. Jackie and Ray had made an adoption album to assist the birth parents in deciding who would be right for their child. "My mom went with me to do this. I don't really remember my dad's reaction to all this because he doesn't share his feelings readily. He's getting better at it, though." Actually John was deeply hurt and disappointed, and needed time to grow close to his new grandson.

There was a prayer ceremony the night Lori gave Barrett to Jackie and Ray. Her pregnancy counselor had reminded her that, "I'd cry buckets of tears, and I remember the handing over ceremony in the hospital. I sure cried then. Everyone did." After Barrett's birth, Lori finished high school, went to college for a year, and then to work full time. She dated several young men, but still had no real girlfriends. She dated another young man for a brief time and got pregnant again. This time she knew and told her mom and brother, Joe, right away. There was less fear but more shame that she'd let this happen again. Lori knew now the feelings of hurt and disappointment in the family but she also knew she wouldn't be banished from the family. "I didn't want to go through this alone as I had much of the first pregnancy. I needed support," she concluded.

"Only once did I hear my mom be really angry. We'd had an argument over something and I went down the basement to get away. I overheard her tell my dad that I was a slut. That really hurt but I felt like I'd sort of brought it on myself. Afterwards, mom said she was sorry and I knew that she was just releasing some of her own feelings. I don't remember much what my dad felt, because he didn't share his feelings as much and was at work much of the time. My mom did all the woman stuff—going to doctor's appointments, asking me how I felt. I felt my dad (as most men) felt somewhat uncomfortable around me when I was pregnant."

"Because I was out of school and working, I considered keeping this baby and raising it myself. Jackie and Ray honestly said they would support any decision I made. They were ready for another addition to their family if I wanted to do another open adoption with them. I knew there was no pressure from them to give them this baby. I was surrounded by wonderful people. My mom was also very honest with me." Marianne again told Lori that she and John did not feel she should raise the baby in their home. There were four younger siblings in the house and if they allowed Lori to raise the baby in their home a lot of the real childrearing responsibilities would fall to Marianne while Lori worked or went back to school. "I was mad at first," Lori recalls, "but realized she was right. She was calling me to responsibility. Eventually I realized that I still was not ready to raise a child. I approached Jackie and Ray and they happily agreed to parent this baby. I went to their house and considered names with them, which we'd not done with Barrett. This time, Jackie went to the doctor's appointments with me. She was with me the first time we heard the baby's heartbeat. Maddie's birth was very painful but Jackie and Ray were in the delivery room with my dad, mom, and me. I liked having them there with me. Dad and Ray filmed the birth. This time the handing over ceremony was not nearly as wrenching. We dressed Maddie together. The first time, we didn't know what we were getting into. This time, I knew these people were not taking my baby away from me. Not really. They are raising her and giving her the life she deserves that I can't give to her. They will still allow me to be a big part of her life. It was not nearly as hard as with Barrett, yet (in another way) it *was* harder because she is a girl. I always liked girl things. But I was excited for Jackie that now she had a daughter. Maddie is everything I'd hope for in a little girl of my own. At this time in my life, I have a few close girl friends." This statement would seem to indicate that Lori connects motherhood and having close girl friends.

During the family discussion on "The Ugly Chair," Lori says that her mom is blind to her kids' faults, "she thinks we're the best." Mom sits in the ugly chair. In the dream, Lori has dark hair. Lori makes reference in other dreams to herself as a "dumb blonde." She may be afraid of others seeing her as a dumb blonde. Because Lori is very pretty and lighthearted, others may not see her depth. Her dark-haired self in this dream is the part of herself that is not flighty; rather it is intuitive, intelligent, yet feels empty. It is Lori looking over the room of her self and deciding to make some changes. Everything in the room is blurry except the "mom's" chair. The chair is of many different colors. *Being in the mother's chair has changed everything!* In the dream, her mother self says to slow down, don't dwell in the past. Start from scratch. Which is what Lori is doing in her current reality. She's dealt with her eating disorder, has been very open about her pregnancies, and is satisfied with the decisions she's made.

Her dream, "On the Run" (BOS11), may indicate that Lori is moving through life trying to get away from her perfectionism and her sense of emptiness. It touches on the dumb blonde image, a very painful way for Lori to name herself. She doesn't know what she's running from, but it is running in a sense of moving on, not of hiding—moving into the future, wanting to know what it holds. Lori knows she wants a husband and realizes that she has learned a lot about men through her experiences. She will not again jump into a relationship too quickly. When the right person comes along she'll know. The seatbelt image of "Cruising" (BOS14) keeps Lori safe. She now has many friendships. She is taking care of herself, although the "dumb blonde" is present to keep her wary. Lori's personal shadow self may very well be her flighty self. She comments, "The dumb blonde image speaks to me of my failure to complete college. I know if I had stayed in college I could be doing work that was much different than I am doing presently. I think I'd like to go into law, or something that is constantly challenging." Lori constantly seeks to turn poor decisions into positive ones.

In the "Same Old Store, Different Look" (BOS27), there are new rooms she has not known before. Although nightmarish, the latter dream indicates an unsettled self which avoids making decisions, yet shows that, in time she will do just that. The treasure dream, "Long Lost" (BOS26), presents the promising results of making good decisions. The symbol of jewelry is an image of the wholeness toward which each of us is always moving. It is *grandmother's* jewelry making it especially valuable. As the brightly colored chair makes the whole room beautiful, so this jewelry can make any outfit beautiful. A promise of wholeness is repeated in the pattern of the circular necklace, bracelet and ring. Lori is taking a step toward wholeness.

The entire family is on the journey to wholeness, on a new path, moving away from its past. Lori's story is the background of the story that is unfolding presently. Perhaps none of these family members would be who they are today if Lori's story hadn't happened. It has caused them to get in touch with themselves, more in touch with their feelings, to grow, and to appreciate themselves as family on new levels.

The Family Shadow

I am upstairs getting ready for the morning and Mom is downstairs cleaning the bathroom. I come down the stairs and turn right. I see in the kitchen a butter bowl (Nu-Maid), and I see a shadow. I go to the other side and I see Mrs. X. standing there. I try to shout to Mom to warn her but nothing comes out (BOS 1, recurring - "Mrs X.," Tess B.).

As Lori takes a fresh turn, almost everything in the Bosch family has returned to being as American and normal as a plastic butter bowl. Relieved, Mom is cleaning the bathroom, cleaning up what has become the family "crap." We have met the family shadow, in Lori's striving for perfection, striving for an impossible ideal image, and have seen it appear in the bodily expression of Lori's eating disorder. Now let us look at three dreams which depict the shadow side of the family with great directness.

Interestingly enough, they come from the two youngest members of the family. What is young and fresh in the family, symbolized in Tess, enters into the kitchen, the place of transformation. The family is now Nu-Maid, although even here there is a worried feeling. It is Tess who picks up another presence, a shadow, a family "member" still not fully recognized. The kids describe Mrs.X, one of their neighbors, as threatening. They perceive her as "psycho," violent, scary, hateful, and threatening. "She's a night prowler," one of them states, "not considerate." She even peeks into the family's windows. But the amazing thing about Mrs. X. is that she "cleans up after everyone," a kind of neighborhood environmentalist. So the dream above begins and ends with a reference to cleaning up.

TABLE 4-1 SAMPLES OF BOSCH FAMILY SHADOW SYMBOLS

Dm #	Dreamer	Symbol	Archetypal or Family Meanings
BOS1	Tess	"Mrs. X"	night prowler; threatening; scary; cleans up after everyone
BOS30	David	someone is trying to rob us	the shadow's power to drain energy until recognized
		Griffin	mythical animal, half eagle, half lion
		black dragon	frightening; powerful
		trampoline	playful aspect of shadow
BOS31	David	shadow to black man	vagueness changes to the more recognizable, yet still unknown
		dead man into	shadow becomes part of who we are
		sandwich	fostering health/growth
		Dad	positive aspect of Shadow; protector moving from mom's chair to dad's chair

What is the meaning of this eccentric, if not outright crazy, neighbor who appears in Tess' dream as a "shadow?" The clear indication of the family shadow provides opportunity to begin a core exploration of this family characteristic. As an inner unacknowledged member of the family, the shadow carries a quality that is threatening to the family view of itself. It is threatening to the point of death.

> *Tess and I are in the backyard of someone, looking towards Griffins' house. . . . I have a BB gun. We look up and see birds in the distance. I shoot at one of them . . . [then] I see a bird coming towards me aiming at the ground. It's getting bigger and bigger. It turns into a black dragon.*
>
> *Next, we're in a house in the basement which has a high ceiling. I'm worrying that Mom's going to kill me. I shot the bird. I'm wondering what I'm going to do with the dead dragon which is also in the room. It's laying in a corner across the room from me.*
>
> *Four boys come in. They examine the dragon. They climb up on the dragon and begin to jump on it like it's a trampoline. I think, "Well, I guess that problem is solved"* (BOS 30, 112197 - The Dragon I Shot, David B.).

The Shadow always seems to be in someone else's backyard, not our own. We want to deny, then to dispatch the threatening, the ugly, or the embarrassing self. In the case of David's dragon dream, it is the *family's* need to fly high, but instead the bird dives right to the ground. It heralds death in some form, but continues in another form among us. First it is a griffin, a bird, a black dragon, then a *dead* black dragon. So even the Shadow undergoes stages of transformation. We find we have power over it if we face it, engage with it, recognize that it is not going away.

It appears constantly in the hidden disguises of power: the griffin, a fabulous animal half-eagle and half-lion; a BB gun, weakly phallic; the bird gets bigger and bigger as the family's ability to fly gets larger and larger. Confronting it brings about the black dragon—the frightening, powerful unknown self. In the unconscious world with its high ceiling, the feminine, mom, knows that we should not kill the dragon. But then the dead dragon awaits resurrection, which the fresh young masculine energy provides. The dragon comes "alive" in the form of the playful power of a trampoline! What has been so feared, has been restored as a source of fun and exercise (See Table 4-2).

> Dad and I are in our dining room and I see a figure that flashes from a shadow to a black man then back to a shadow. He has a rope around his neck. He is dead. I think I'm the one who killed him. We keep the dead man in the room. He is seated on the dining room chair where Mom usually sits by the doorway.
>
> Mom keeps trying to get me to eat the man. She just keeps asking me over and over. Mom brings me parts of him that are ground up like hamburger.
>
> Next I am sitting in the family room in Dad's big, blue chair. Mom walks in with a sandwich on a plate. I grab the sandwich and I'm ready to eat it and then I say, "You put him in there" (BOS 31, 112297 - I Hung A Shadow, David B.).

Jung's concept of the Shadow, as a developing aspect of the psyche, moves through defined stages. The first is a familiar one: the stage of the unknown, undeveloped trait which, being undeveloped, is awkward and inconvenient and frightening. It can and does "trip us up." In the second stage, after having received some respect and acceptance, the shadow becomes re-creative, even cathartic. It is the playful trampoline. It is in its final stage that the Shadow is least known or acknowledged. What is first met as a dark aspect of the soul has through pain and suffering been transformed into the recreative, then the mystical state, the state of wholeness and completion.

It is clear from the journey with Lori that the family has undergone a change. It—they—have moved from ignorance of an unknown member of the family, the shadow of a demanding perfectionism, to recognition of its presence. Acceptance of its nature has opened up to acknowledgement of this trait, in fact, to "prop it up" and let it remain among them. They have permitted themselves to play with it, permitting its lighter side to begin to develop. Ingesting the Shadow, however, already announces that the family, although wary, must let this "person" become totally integrated into themselves. It has the power to provide health and lead them to the mystical.

The nature of the paschal mystery unfolds among the members of the Bosch family as they suffer the "death" of their original idea of the perfect Catholic image. Lori's story has become their story, and that family story has opened vital developments among them as it has impacted the lives of others. In their flawed history they increasingly discover the vitality of their authentic identity.

The Path of Family Transformation

The path the family has walked is the same path of transformation outlined in the development of every maturing adult. It moves from shadow and death toward hope, and culminates in "treasures." This path occurs not only in the history of every intentional religious group, but also in *any* group that becomes defined as a distinct entity. On the day that the Bosch family explored the Path of Transformation (see Figure 4-1) as a family movement, they reached into their memory of the affective nature of their experiences. They recognized that Lori's pregnancies upset the stability of their family life and perspectives. Efforts to keep things quiet, beginning with Lori, could not save them from dying to their assumptions of themselves as family. Moral and religious questions have had to be faced. Lori came into a new awareness of what her parents, for all their support, could not do for her. She had thrust herself onto an adult plane, a place of no reversal.

As each member named his or her feelings, words came forth: *denial, livid, devastated, anger, confusion, afraid, grief.* These profound emotions were complex. At the beginning of the first pregnancy, Marianne and John had to confront the grief and hurt at what they felt was Lori's betrayal of their beliefs and expectations. By the end of the pregnancy, the intense experience of helping Lori make a good decision, the awareness of this new little person, Barrett, who was already becoming a part of their family soul, led them into a deeper grief. How could they let go of Barrett? He seemed already a part of them. Knowing that, by open adoption, Barrett would continue to be a part of them barely assuaged the terrible pain of that farewell ritual. Both had experienced the aloneness which comes in a dying process.

Marianne's support led to hours with Lori, going to appointments with doctors and social workers. John must often have felt isolated from that women's world as he went off to the pharmacy to continue his support by working there. Joe was about to go to Germany for a year of study when he learned of the second pregnancy. He remembers that his first level of anger was aimed at "Lori's stupidity" but then he recognized a second level of anger. How could he miss being with the family as they again traversed new territory?

Although releasing Maddie to Jackie and Ray was much easier, it was a repeat—a deepening—of the dying process. Things would never be the same, even as they looked to the future with joy and pride at the decisions they had made, resulting in their new union of hearts. Especially Marianne, John, and Lori recognized the value of what they accomplished over those years of trauma, uncertainty, and now new steps forward. Lori herself could name her determination to see life differently, to make choices based on convictions and values.

FIGURE 4-1

THE BOSCH FAMILY PATH OF TRANSFORMATION

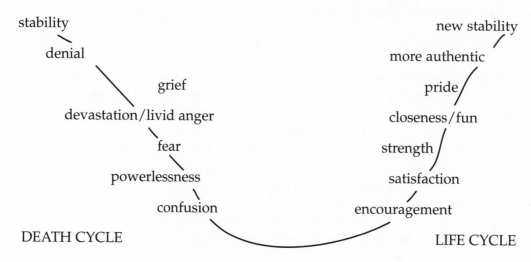

DEATH CYCLE   LIFE CYCLE

Who are we now as a family?

How have relationships changed?

Where do we access a new sense of power?

People ask Lori what it's like to have a family through open adoption. She finds such a family hard to describe, recognizing its members as being different from cousins or little brothers and sisters. The shaping of new family routines began as Christmas and Easter celebrations increasingly blended the two families: Ray and Jackie and Barrett and Maddie and Lori and Marianne and John and Joe and Johnny and Tess and David. Slowly, the new patterns began to settle in. Lori, now adult, had become independent, having her own apartment and a job; but even more, she was dealing with her eating habits, and seeing the seductive nature of her eating disorder. As in every transformation, three elements express the movement and the change which occurs. The identity of the family has moved from a sure but incomplete ideal, through breakdown and confusion, and into a search for a new life. Relationships have shifted within and outside the family. A new and truer sense of themselves is beginning to come forth.

What words do they *now* use to name themselves? *"Encouragement, strength, fun, closeness, pride, more authentic."* These are more than words, they are the feelings which describe the vitality they find among themselves. Now these feelings are carried within many dimensions and expressions of the ever-present reality of their family shadow. In their transformation process the Bosch family have suffered the death of their "perfect" image and been re-born into a new identity, with new relationships, and a new sense of inner power.[31]

In a final reflection exercise the family raised images that each felt best expressed their identity as family. Tess' image of a car, moving on the highway but never alone, got a strong family response, as did Joe's big, fluffy colorful couch. But a surprise grabbed their imagination when Marianne told the story of the oak tree in their front yard, a story they had never heard.

TABLE 4-2 BOSCH FAMILY TRANSFORMATION SYMBOLS

Dm #	Dreamer	Symbol	Archetypal or Family Meanings
BOS1	Tess	kitchen	room where raw material becomes edible nourishing food
		cleaning	from Mom (bathroom) to Mrs. X, the shadow who cleans up the neighborhood
BOS13	Johnny	kitchen	transformation
BOS5	Lori	ugly chair	"mom" presence brings new perspective to brightly colored chair
BOS7	Marianne	small path	from fear to power
BOS9	John	toward a wedding	from walking to riding; a sudden turn
BOS20	John	walking	from alone to with people
BOS14	Lori	walking	from "this neighborhood" to a gas station, new energy
BOS19	Marianne	wall surface	from levels of covering down to the original authentic structure
BOS23	Johnny	store	from work to play
BOS27	Lori	Biggs	old store to one with new rooms
BOS30	David	black dragon	from powerful attacker to recreational trampoline: playful aspect of shadow
BOS31	David	shadow	transformation from unknown to known
		dead man sandwich	potential to source of energy integrating the shadow

When Marianne and John were a much younger couple they had gone deep into the woods alongside their house. It was a time before development had surrounded them with suburbia. They spotted an oak tree, a young sapling, and dug it up. They brought it out of the woods and planted it in their front yard, thus opening up the empty landscape. In the years since, the tree has grown deep roots and has flourished. Now the oak tree in its solid presence is much like the "original, real, authentic log cabin." And it is theirs! "I have nothing to hide," Lori said when she concluded her story. There are no more family layers to pull back. The tree has grown strong. They have pruned it and it provides beauty and protection from the sun. It is always before them.

The Original, Real Log Cabin: The Authentic Family Soul

The "mom" and "sister" of the institutional Church are still part of the Bosch family relationship, but the family no longer listens to the "shoulds and oughts" of that conversation. They have discovered that God's life in them is SO MUCH MORE than these. Marianne's comment on her opening dream reflects the family reality: "At this time of my life, I choose to listen more deeply to the 'old house' part of myself—that part which contains age old wisdom that's always been a part of me."

"I can hardly put this awareness into words. But I have a deep sense that God calls me to a more WHOLE understanding that every human community to which I belong will be flawed. They are not perfect and as such cannot love or be loved perfectly. There is only one perfect being: God. And God's love is so beyond anything I can understand. I believe God is in me and others in the community. But God is also beyond the community. God's love is just BIGGER, GREATER. I think that it is in embracing this concept that I experience my FAITH. My community is where I choose to live out, to express my faith, but it is not my faith. My faith is in God."

TABLE 4-3 BOSCH FAMILY (TREASURE) WHOLENESS SYMBOLS

Dm #	Dreamer	Symbol	Archetypal or Family Meanings
BOS4	Johnny	Smashing Pumpkins song	strong beautiful feelings
BOS12	Marianne	green book	sense of advancing, maturing
BOS17	Joe	screened-in porch	everything is beautiful, full
		orange geraniums	orange: the red of passion and yellow of wisdom; color of change
BOS21	Joe	cherry wood	large, precious chest; a kind of shrine
BOS26	Lori	Grand-mother's jewel box	ring with brown colored stone, matching bracelet and necklace
BOS27	Marianne	log cabin	all the outer layers are gone; down to the original, authentic, REAL log cabin. It is mine!

The last part of the dream carries a kind of exultant joy in Marianne's recognition of the authentic and the real. "In fact, it excites me. I KNOW that THIS IS THE TREASURE—the discovery that God is within me and all around me. God is in the rough, the everyday, the unexpected, the brightly wrapped, the ordinary. In everything. In everyone. God already has the job of being perfect—we don't need to be."

Section B

THE DREAM PROCESS

CHAPTER FIVE

Transformation and Community

We have seen a family moving very directly through a transformation. Its members are increasingly aware of their movement from an unknown, shadowy identity toward a new and more conscious recognition of themselves as a family. This movement unfolds as the family carries out a formidable task that launches it into greater inner power as a group of persons. What each one undertook alone—and all undertook together—to support Lori, propelled them into their next stage of a life transition. Marianne's life journey had been a "peaceful walk" with an eager sense of getting "home," until she was confronted with an alarming animal—*fear*—causing her to put down her personal power. Only by reclaiming her power, her voice, by walking with her masculine principle, and her *"own* dog," could she move on:

> *I am approaching a big, lovely, <u>old</u> home, probably 100-150 years old. . . . I am eager to get there. I see a small path that, although it is a bit out of the way, will lead me. . . . The path meanders through the trees. Fallen leaves are all along the path. It is very inviting. . . .*
> *I begin to walk, feeling very peaceful and enjoying the beauty of nature, when suddenly, I hear a deep growl. Uh-oh, a dog—and not a friendly one. . . . Slowly I lay down my purse and begin to move back the way I came. The (yellow) dog walks parallel with me growling the whole time.*
> *I make it safely to (my) dream group and tell everyone my story. As we begin to settle down, . . . I anxiously await permission to go get my purse. I begin to*

feel nervous, hesitant, apprehensive as I realize that I am going to have to SPEAK UP (if) I am going to get my purse. I am also quite fearful of going out there by that damn dog again! I do speak up and I do go get my purse but I don't go alone.. . . .

Besides the man that goes with me, I think I also take my own dog which overpowers the yellow dog. I feel very secure in my mission with these two by my side (BOS 7, 102797 - The Barking Dog, Marianne B.).

By its nature every pathway, every journey, has a beginning, middle, and ending. John, too, "walks" alone, and he, too, meets other parts of himself, "talking with people along the way" (BOS20). He is provided with the role of the one who uses a "Cross pen," both an instrument of competence and of faith. He uses this to encourage communication in the family, which he admitted at one of our brunch meetings is difficult. And in one of David's dreams,

[We] are climbing stairs along a huge highway . . . we pass lots of people, . . . All of a sudden the highway is gone but the steps are still going up into mid air. To keep going we have to walk around a cage (BOS 33, 112397 - The Steps, David B.).

For David, as for the others, new capacities needed to be used as the journey changed dramatically.

Rooms, also, are a common household image that summarize the family transformation. Both Tess and Johnny have kitchen dreams. The kitchen is an archetypal image of raw material being changed into edible nourishment, and of food in its transformation changing into an integral part of the body tissue. For Tess, while "Mom is cleaning the bathroom," Tess goes downstairs and sees in the kitchen a "NU-Maid" butter bowl—even though the Shadowy Mrs. X. is just around the corner. This ordinary American family must deal with its shadow self in the process of becoming "NU-Maid." Johnny also has a dream indicating that the kitchen offers food and drink to help the family move beyond the present situation.

So we see the dreams functioning as descriptors of ongoing transformation and providing clues for guidance. The communal dream process for opening awareness and attention developed over a period of years while, with each new experimenting community, steps of community dream work became clarified and refined. These steps are not completely different from the ordinary person's procedure for opening one's spirit to the action of God.

A time or moment of transformation can never be forced, however, only prepared for. Dr. Tom Dyehouse, who brings his particular skill in Gestalt therapy to dream therapy, suggests that:

The idea of *storming heaven* through hard diligent work and effort can lead to an effete, conservative expression of an athletic religiosity associated with the Western work *ethic*. . . . Likewise, the attitude of, 'Relax, there's nothing you can do about it. It's all out of your control' will lead to an effete, childlike attitude that is destined to leave you stranded inside the slavery of your small, ego self, . . . The obvious solution lies somewhere in a paradoxical integration. . . . For this, you must work and prepare. If you (do this) steadfastly with careful attention and without anxiety or *reactive* effort, you too can return to the Source, while you are yet living.[32]

This describes the quality of the process that incurs both psychological sweat and playful reception. This attitude is inherent to the moral and spiritual character associated with transformative growth. So in our dream experiments, groups soon realized that they had to move through transformation in defined stages.

Discovering a Transformation in Process

A community family, who moved into a neighborhood house 3 or 4 years ago, is finally getting around to cleaning out the basement of the house. It is full of junk from earlier years, as well as some of their own things which are piled on top.

Several community members are helping clean out the basement. We have taken their good things out and put them up in the house where they can be used. This is possible because of work that has been done in the house recently. Now we are working to carry out the old stuff, packing large items in boxes and picking up bits and pieces with shovels, brooms and dustpans.

Finally, we get down to the basement floor. In some places, it is irregular, even bumpy. We begin working on these areas, cleaning them more intensively to find out what the bumps are. As we clean, we make a discovery. At first we can't believe it because it is so startling: these are human bodies! Strangely, the bodies are apparently being slowly pushed up from the earth. It is as if they are oozing up into our hands as we kneel on the floor dumbfounded.

We hold them reverently. Who are they? How did they get there? What should we do with them? We ask ourselves these questions, but don't know the answers (NJ Dream 79.012690 - Cleaning the Basement, Jeff R.).

This New Jerusalem dream is one of many in which images of the unconscious appear. Here, in the earthy basement of the unconscious, *something* is literally oozing to the surface. What is happening?

A transformation is happening! When such a metamorphosis occurs, it includes a disintegration of the past. It is usually accompanied by loss and grief, since leaving the familiar is seldom painless. The references to "cleaning" and "three or four years" would indicate that the New Jerusalem community is still clearing up the reactions associated with our founder's leaving for another ministry. In their projections on him and on one another, they have collected much "junk" that needs to be discarded—"their own stuff." Valuing and saving the rich teachings and communal history that their lifestyle developed, they "have taken their good things out and put them up . . . where they can be used."[33] Transformation includes a transition moment where nothing is clear, all is confusing: "We ask ourselves these questions. We don't know the answers." The individual or group may work at an "identity," but nothing yet rings true until discovery heralds insight.

On a broader level, the images of the buried human bodies may point to the non-ordained lay persons who comprise the community. They are, in fact, the Church's substance, its foundation—hierarchical though its more visible structure may be. As long as community members continue to depend solely on the gifts, the leadership, the education of their ordained leaders, it is possible to deny, repress, or bury their own responsibilities as mature Christians. To live in this state is to deny the necessity not only of responsibility but of conversion. In the dream, the workers' spiritual curiosity urges them to unearth the buried, bumpy, and irregular human potential within their community and their Church.

Transformation is, thus, a movement through death to new life. What had been buried so deeply at the time of the dream? Apparently the community had to remove much superfluous material to discover what was "oozing up." They had to bring "it" to consciousness before they could touch and reverence the most deeply buried aspect of themselves. They seem to be touching and reverencing the very nature of their humanness itself, the humanness belonging to the entire Church. They are rightly dumbfounded. The dreamers themselves were dumbfounded by the symbols in this dream.

The Relationship of Transformation to Symbol

Human communities express their life through symbol. Symbol, however, is to be distinguished from sign. Jung defines a symbol as:

> an *indefinite* expression with *many meanings*, pointing to something not easily defined and not fully known; whereas, the sign always has a *fixed meaning* because it is a conventional abbreviation for, or a commonly accepted indication of, something known.[34]

At best the symbol serves as an embodiment of the human spirit. The whirling dervish of ancient Persian communities dances the whole cosmos into life. The drum, calling card of primitive tribes, announces the "masculine" to our latter day sophisticated society. The graphic designer presents a corporate client with a new logo. In each case, image and symbol are in action. When the human spirit, limited by mere words, is in despair or exultation, it moves to the body/sensate language of symbol. Our desperate efforts to contact and express our deepest longings and wildest hopes bring us to the core of our being, which is often *incommunicado* except for the medium of the inner and outer senses. Such sounds and movements as those of drum or dance make the human spirit tangible.

On the one hand, we humans consciously shape our communal rituals and symbols; on the other hand, symbols which have become part of the group's understanding of itself shape the community. They catalyze and energize the life within it. The religious *intentional* community participates, it seems to me, even more in the highly symbolic life. For a Catholic Christian, for example, this is most obvious where there is a vitality of sacraments. Sacraments are outward signs of inner power, yet the renewal of our church systems has only begun to break through the stagnation and ennui which have encrusted our life of ritual. Central to Carl Jung's investigation of the human psyche is his understanding of this role of symbol in religious experience.[35] He states that symbol gives meaning in the unprovable and mysterious dimensions of the unconscious life. Symbols *take hold* of us, *happening* to us, lifting us from the mundane to the *unus mundi*, "the union of our wholeness with the potential world of the first creation, the eternal Ground of all being." In this we "escape from the stifling grip of a one-sided view of the world."[36]

Still the question persists, *by what right may we claim that a dream symbol belongs to the entire community?* Every dream has *many* layers. One of these is a community layer. Just as a sculpture may be viewed from three hundred and sixty different degrees, providing three hundred and sixty different views, and still remain the same sculpture, so the dream has multiple layers of meaning, all of which may be valid without disagreeing with one another. Or we might consider the hologram in the same way: a three-dimensional photographic negative, only one angle of which can be seen at a time; yet, any one piece of the negative produces the entire picture.

The multiple layers of meaning in a dream are much like that. Jeremy Taylor states, in fact, that there is no such thing as only one layer of meaning, specifically because the dream describes the *whole* person. Every major "angle" of our human-ness is expressed in a dream: personality, interior life, sexual desire, physical health, work, relationships, and so on.[37] As members of various groups worked and played with dreams, I came first to realize and then to expect that, for members of an intentional group, this community layer of a dream is present and identifiable.

Understanding "tribal" dreams—and therefore, the actions and rituals arising out of them—is gained by communal recognition. Although layers of varied signif-icance are often recognized, members do not often find the differing reflections dis-agreeing with one another. Perhaps this union of meaning is attributable to the common humanness from which it arises. This is Carl Jung's fundamental under-standing of archetypes—that is, basic patterns of common human experience. At times of puzzlement or curiosity about a specific dream image, the discerners are wise to seek out the ancient archetypal mythologies—whether secular or scriptur-al—which are related to it. The shape and form of the collective psyche repeatedly become clarified, rising up from its hidden place within the larger unconscious of the Church and humankind.

The desire of a family or community for transformation and conversion is at the heart of listening to their dreams. Just as an individual person may seek trans-formation by tapping the unconscious, so may each community, or tribe, enter its

73

collective unconscious, finding there the archetypal images and symbols that have power to change it. In the deep stream of the collective unconscious old memories connect us to all of human life: its countless rebirths, its evolutionary growth, its struggle to open up the potential to bring about a kind of mutation. All is there in collective humanity. The effect of transformation in each person is individuation, the process by which one draws strength from the collective experience, breaks from it, and becomes a distinct and unique being. Groups, too, being made up of individuals, go through transformation.[38] The question for the tribe—as for the individual within it—is whether it will make a choice for *collective* individuation, specifying its identity, or will be swept along by the mass consciousness of the group or the culture. This will depend on the extent to which the individuals that comprise it grow in spiritual and moral stature.[39]

As a new millennium begins, the rising awareness of myth and ritual as means of empowerment is enabling many to reclaim resources of nature and experience, still half buried in the forgetfulness of the human journey. It is a time for re-discovering the joyous capacities we share as humans as well as for confronting our darkness. Many renewal communities among Christian churches are in the process of reclaiming freedom through an entire list of symbolic vehicles: image, music, body gesture, dance, color, word, and much more. The ancient chariot of the dream arrives fairly fresh upon our symbolic horizon. Not to be ignored is information from the flow of energy associated with body work, natural materials like stones and crystals, and the growing understanding of the human capacity to direct inner resources toward affecting the outer world, as occurs most notably in healing. We see this modeled by Jesus as he reminds us that those who have faith will carry out even greater works than his (John 15:120).

Engagement with a transformative experience often concludes with delight and astonishment, as the symbol or metaphor that triggered the transformation re-integrates possibilities and capacities with original myths and stories. The path of personal or communal conversion is always one of disintegration, re-grounding, and re-integration. For New Jerusalem, this transformation is indicated in its movement from a clerical-led Catholic group to one now struggling with the implications of non-ordained leadership amidst a constantly shifting religious culture. For traditional religious communities, the transformation is a contemporary re-played version of their historical renewals of past centuries. For a family, it may well be confronting the shadow, killing it, or finding a new way to resurrect it as a part of themselves. Symbol, related to myth and story and dreams, has a primary role to play in this ongoing process of transformation. Mircea Eliade tells us:

> The symbol, the myth, and the image are the very substance of the spiritual life . . . they may become disguised, mutilated, or degraded, but never are extirpated.[40]

Enacting NJ Dream 44, <u>The Vestments Are the Treasure</u>

Spring Symbol Celebration: From the depths of the unconscious the pulsation of the masculine and feminine is always heard.

Spring Symbol Celebration: The Tree of Life is made from the personal symbols of its members.

Spring Symbol Celebration: Call to the Poor Gate (writing letters to our Congress-persons).

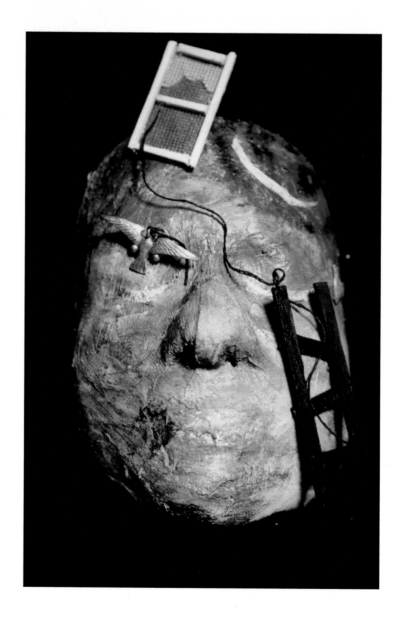

Masks reveal the soul of the family or the group.

Smooth, unbroken path,
suddenly interrupted--
new music begins...

Mandala of Personal Transformation: As a singer looses her voice and
learns new lessons before it returns. Lynn McClellan

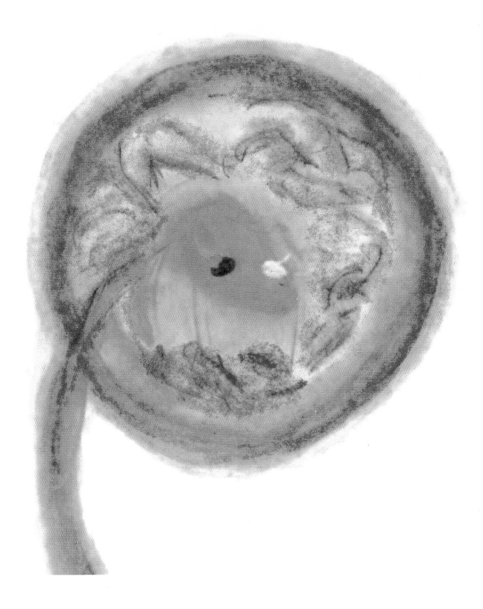

The transferring of life through the Ursuline umbilical cord, 1995.
Mary-Cabrini Durkin

Familiar Arenas of Effective Symbols

Various ways to express and record transforming symbols have long been known and celebrated consciously in all kinds of families and communities. Any list doubtless will be arbitrary to some extent. Categories include in some form archetypes which have had a catalyzing effect on groups, or which have provided a place for expressing the currents of life that rise and fall within community, family or group rhythms. Since archetypes are countless, it is helpful to recognize more generic arenas. The fact that traditional areas of symbols have appeared in the tribal dreams described, emphasizes their importance in the collective psyche of the tribal members.

An example of a category of importance is the name and charism which identify the spirituality of the group. Naming ceremonies appear among the most ancient of tribes. Although baptismal rites among Christians have kept alive ceremonial celebrations accompanying the naming process, it is pre-literate tribes for whom naming is an opportunity to *assign an identity* related to a trait, a role, or a vision had by the person named. For communities, too, names carry energy and meaning. Unlike many church parishes burdened with an episcopal choice for a distant Roman saint, intentional communities tend to choose their own designation from a communal experience of the Spirit of God, or from a sense of destiny. The name of a church community is often expressed in the common ministry.

A clear example is presented in the history of the first Sisters of Saint Joseph. They chose their name in order to honor Saint Joseph, the husband of Mary and the father of Jesus Christ. They perceived in him a model for both their lifestyle and pattern of interior holiness. In fact, at the entrance to the beautiful cemetery in Nazareth, there is a unique *bas relief.* Here Joseph is depicted not as a carpenter but as a dreamer, lying and sleeping, one hand over his ear, as though listening for God's voice! It's no wonder that the group of sisters who undertook a dream experiment to prepare for Chapter had a dreamer's name to rely on. Through their dreams, the sisters got in touch with much of Joseph's character, naming it humility, service, hospitality, and providing for the needs of the moment. This name has stood the test of inspiration for well over two hundred years. Joseph is a saint for whom many groups have been named, a name which calls Christians to look closely at Joseph's life and to respond to him as a model of the New Testament prophet, living a simple working person's life, and remaining faithful in time of confusion and mystery.

The Ursulines, no less dreamers than Joseph's sisters, reach for their name from deep within a Norse moon goddess myth—a goddess attended by eleven thousand stars.[41] This myth evolved within the story of the sixth century Ursula, who inspired sixteenth century Angela Merici to identify the women gathered around her as the Company of Saint Ursula. The historical details around Ursula are shaky, but key information provides the legend of a woman who led eleven women (some say 11,000), personally committed to Christ, on a pilgrimage from the British Isles to some holy site. A storm swept them ashore among Huns, who slew them because of their fidelity to their chosen state of virginity. In Christian art Ursula is often depicted as a Viking-like heroine: strong, self-confident, the virgins enfolded in her large cloak. The narrative makes no mention of dependence on male leadership, which may explain Angela's choice. The sixteenth-century Company was the first major Catholic community of women founded without the protection of male leadership, committed to sailing forth into the world with only their own promise of virginity. Perhaps many contemporary Ursuline women would be further amazed to know that an even more ancient mythological basis for their name comes from an animal, the bear, *ursa*, which carries the symbolic meaning of the caring mother. The bear knows instinctively when to hibernate, what foods to eat after months in the cave, and how to protect its young.[42] Thus a name as symbol may have its roots in the most instinctual aspects of life, moving through historical periods, and continuing to have transformative power and meaning all the way into contemporary times.

For the small lay community being formed in Cincinnati, the name of the heavenly City, as New Jerusalem is described in the Book of Revelation, was received with delight and assurance. They had been called to a *city* neighborhood, hoping to make a start in carrying out the scriptural promise that "I see the holy city, the New Jerusalem. Here God lives among humankind. . . . They shall be his people, and he will be their God: his name will be God-with-them . . . there will be no more death, and no more weeping or sadness. The world of the old order has gone" (Rev. 21:3-4).

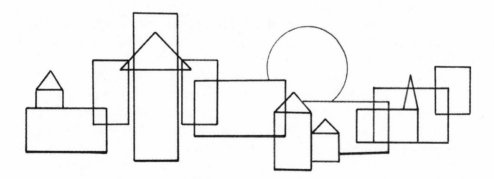

In the following chapters we will continue to apply the transformation experience to other symbolic expressions such as: nature symbols, sacrament and ritual, body as symbol, service to the poor, art and its forms, and transforming images that are unique to a particular community. Let us list the six steps leading to the transformations that developed through the dream experiments, each adaptable to a particular group, or optional. These steps, also to be discussed in the following chapters, are:

1. A Beginning Time - a time of reflection, education, preparing to dream and establishing timing;
2. A Facilitators Day - a time to train facilitators of larger groups, an optional step if the group is small;
3. Dream Discernment Days - days when the entire group enters into the "sweat" of identifying images and common dreams, of categorizing the images into patterns;
4. Identification and Development of Theme Statements;
5. Theological Reflection and Forming of Directional Statements;
6. Honoring the Source of the Dream by Ritual and/or Actions.

CHAPTER SIX

Preparing For and Collecting the Dreams

Preparation for a Tribal Dream Project

What is involved in the preparation for collective dreaming? Although the processes parallel those of individual dreaming, the nature of multiple "souls" forming one collective soul presents technical as well as theoretical difficulties. Even the size of one group compared to another raises the challenge of using different strategies. The size of the group, as we discovered in the case of a family dreaming together, affects the degree of formality and the style of applying any strategies.

Most of the steps listed below may apply to either personal or the communal dream work and play, if we accept that within these general strategies there is necessity for flexibility and constant revision of form unique to the group. Instruction will be a first step for almost all those who agree to enter the place of the collective psyche. As a program director I have found the following points to provide a firm and essential basis if the work is to be completed. They can be presented orally or by way of written material, with individual packets available for all potential participants. The packets would contain the following:

1. A RATIONALE FOR ACCEPTING TRIBAL DREAMS

This includes five areas that provide helpful background for many persons: a) reminders of our scriptural roots and the dreams that appear there as messages to God's people through an individual; b) acknowledgment of the symbolic power in Christian sacraments and liturgy; c) some background in the Jungian perspective on the collective psyche, or tribal soul; d) notice of the effect of tribal dreams among primitive groups; and, e) attention to contemporary writings about experiences with group dreaming.

2. BASIC PRINCIPLES OF DREAM WORK/DREAM PLAY

The renewal movements within spirituality, and the current hunger for significance in a chaotic world, have fostered an interest in the study of dreams; therefore, much readable material is available, and a bibliography should be included in the material offered for dream preparation.[43] Recognizing, however, that in any group some people will just be beginning to confront the mystery of dreams, a clear yet complete handout of basic principles should be included in a packet for each potential participant. In Section C I have provided a sample of some simple directives which are adaptable for various groups.[44]

3. A PROPOSED PLAN OF ACTION

The proposed plan of action will have been worked out in conjunction with members of the community who have either initiated the project for their tribe, or have interests and skills which have drawn them into the planning. It will include a suggested calendar indicating the stages by which the venture will progress. This action will also indicate a way by which the entire group or the organizing team will choose a significant date, or dates, for dreaming.

4. THE IMPORTANCE AND MANNER OF RECORDING THE DREAMS

Journaling is a classic discipline of the interior life, as any collection of journals, daybooks, autobiographies, diaries and poetic reflections indicates. This is not, however, to diminish the value of recording the dream through art, some body movement, or other varied and less rational expressions. The word to be underlined here is *record*! Some participants may need encouragement to understand the need and importance of this step for remembering and later working and playing with the dream.

An equally crucial aspect of this for communal work will call for deciding the kind of records the *group* wants to keep, and who will be responsible for them. Frequently, people less sure of their dreaming capacity will offer to do this organizing and secretarial piece for others—and then be delighted to discover they also have dreams of their own to bring! Clear details about to whom, where, when, and how to submit dreams will encourage members to do just that.

The approaches may vary as widely as the groups, themselves. Joseph's Sisters distributed instructional tapes and printed material to their membership. There was thorough organization of materials and guidance at each step, which never faltered for the whole year. On the other hand, the Bosch family, sitting around the dining room table on a Sunday morning, made their plans and set their dates together. When it came time to search out common themes and recognize repeated images, they formed three small groups: Dad and David worked on images of the masculine and made lists of opposites; Marianne and Joe explored house and body images; and Lori collaborated with Tess and Johnny on Shadow and feminine images with special attention to feelings in the dreams. Tucking their dream tasks amid the family schedule, scattered through various rooms in the house, the family members dug in deep and brought up family discoveries.

5. SUGGESTED PRAYERS OR RITUALS FOR GETTING STARTED

Much that we do as dream work or dream play (as in prayer itself) is to call ourselves to attention, or to trigger awareness. A fresh and creative ritual incorporating word, gesture and some symbolic object, may be the best possible preparation for calling forth a dream. This may be carried out as individual prayer or by a group within the community, or even by the entire group itself. It alerts the soul of each to expect to remember a dream, to trust, and to not judge what comes.

A cluster of Joseph's sisters living in Detroit traveled to their motherhouse near Kalamazoo, Michigan, for the dream night. This place holds the motherlode of myth, tradition and history for them. After gathering to share an evening meal and conversation, they proceeded to the long hall containing their sleeping rooms. Taking a well-decorated dream catcher with them, they visited each one's room, blessed it with the dream catcher, and prayed with her for good dreams that night. Another older occupant emerged from her room, responding to the joyful sounds of the ragtag procession moving down the hall. What was happening? Immediately she received an invitation to join them in blessing her room, her bed, and herself. With delight the sister accepted and her space became "prepared" for the dream message of the night.

Such simple group prayer can energize and inform the spirit of one who may have bypassed the dream project or assumed—as many do—that s/he would not receive a dream. In each community such rituals are developed and adapted uniquely for the nature and size of the group. The minimum requirement usually includes the above elements, but presented in different ways within each unique time structure. Because, as program director, I was able to be present and engaged in the daily community life of New Jerusalem, the preparation was carried out regularly over the year of the study. This was done by way of oral teaching, regular entries in the weekly bulletin, meetings with smaller groups, or just bumping into a questioning community member before worship services on Sunday. A regular part of this process, used in no other experiment, was an agreement to dream on a particular day once a month for a full year. It seemed important, in this case, to open our souls to the energy of a nature event, so we chose the night of the new moon, valuing the significance of "new life" which it symbolized.

On the monthly evening of the dreaming there was a sense of being together even as, in our separate homes, we did our individual preparation for sleep. In order to focus this attention communally, the discerning group formulated a quest, a kind of open "wondering," or a seeking for a response from on high. The quest for August 31, 1989, was the beginning event and we directed our quest as follows: GIVE US INSIGHT INTO THIS DREAM PROCESS AND INTO THE ONGOING LIFE OF NEW JERUSALEM. Nine dreams were collected which provided a delightful surprise. There was a pattern of repeated birth images: "two women are giving birth" (NJ2), two other dreams contain birth canal images, and there is one reference to "waking from our sleeping bags" (NJ5). Those who worked with the dreams felt this birthing indeed described what was happening in the community life. It was coming to life after a long hard community dying. The birth images continued for several months in terms of "eggs hatching," "an egg being painted white," pregnant women, and even a man—Saint Francis—"writhing in labor and giving birth to many little Francises."

What the merging of each quest and response did for the process was to expose another question, another "wondering." So, in the second month, our quest was: September 29, 1989: HOW DO WE ASSIST THE BIRTH PROCESS? SHOW US HOW TO YIELD TO THE STRETCHING PAIN OF BRINGING FORTH NEW LEADERSHIP. In this manner the group was led from month to month, our quests arising from the dream images of the month before. We deliberately chose two months in which *not* to formulate a quest, to test whether it was constricting or controlling the unconscious. In each case, there was a clear pattern which emerged, the sense of a message which resonated within the context of the community journey. As far as could be ascertained, the quest neither controlled nor constricted what inevitably arose as common threads of meaning. This monthly rhythm had the effect of keeping alive a sense of expectancy and awareness that rejuvenated preparation for dreaming.

For the other long-term dream designs in Nazareth, Michigan and in Bruno, Saskatchewan, distance prevented my functioning in this way; rather, delegated committees of the community communicated with me, and transferred the recommended plans for preparation to the group. In the case of Joseph's sisters, small cluster groups met regularly in and around Michigan state. These clusters provided a natural arena for learning, in this situation, using the printed material and audio tape of instructions that were sent to each group. The learning opportunity motivated discussion and solidarity for this rather unusual shared purpose: to prepare for their annual Chapter meeting by dreaming!

The Bruno Ursulines had an even more specific goal for the Chapter of April, 1998, before they contacted me in the early fall of 1996. The aim of this small community of forty persons was large: to decide their future as a community. Were they to merge with another group? To dissolve? To move to another location better suited to their needs and their ministries?

Different than the long-term experiments referred to above, the other Ursuline experiences described in Chapter Two might be called "one-night stands." For the Ursuline Convocation workshop, the Brown County Ursulines had had one dream night that became the source for a two-hour workshop. Within the workshop the preparation was reduced to about twenty minutes! The attendees applied these dreams of one Ursuline community to their own Ursuline congregation, much as one might apply a scriptural passage to one's own situation. The Way of Life group chose to dream as a spontaneous response to "being stuck" in their reflection process; however, they were so affected by the four dreams collected that they took their experience to the larger body of the Ursuline Society of which they were a part.

Collecting the Dreams

Collecting the dreams includes organizing the manner of receiving the dreams, recording and storing them with related materials, and making clear arrangements about who is responsible for each task.

1. The first step is *receiving*. Members need to understand where to send or mail the dreams and who will receive them.
2. The second step calls for creating a simple system of *recording*. Filing, establishing a numbering arrangement, or calling for computer and secretarial skills are included here. This is often where ownership of the project grows. The fruit of the dream work can be lost without the organizational skills of typists, computer-skilled operators, and communicators.

Beyond the visionaries who look into the meanings of a dream and who playfully enter the dream with art, dance, song (or any other form of art) discerners and facilitators design and manage the exchange of interpretation when images are not immediately understandable. The energy generated by dreaming encourages everyone to find a place within the "work" of the dream project.

Communicating With the Membership

I am in the dining room of my parents' home. While my mother is setting the table, I am working above her at the chandelier. I am standing on a chair, or a stepladder, trying to untangle a mess of Christmas lights that SHE had put up with some other lights that I had put up. It's a big mess of tangled lights and wires.

As I'm working, my father comes into the room and says, "Get down from up there!" I try to explain what I'm doing, . . . (and) I stop working to talk with him. He gets angry and says, "Well, you're driving me crazy up there. You shouldn't be doing that. You'll get hurt! Now come down." His words anger me then, because I get the message that . . . I'm not capable of the task, and shouldn't even attempt it. Still not coming down I say, "Dad, I'm not a little girl, I'm a grown woman. The ceilings in my house are much higher than this and I've painted them—changed light bulbs lots of times."

My mother, still working on the dinner table, tells me to stop arguing and just come down for dinner. I do come down then, but am very frustrated at both of them. As (we) sit down, I say, "All right then, but we won't have any lights for dinner now" (NJ Dream 75.022590.K - <u>Changing the Light Bulbs</u>, Carol M.).

Occasionally, as facilitator, I would attach to New Jerusalem's weekly bulletin a Community Dream Project Newsletter indicating the "messages" received in response to a particular request of the Lord. This vehicle would point out themes or patterns that appeared or continued month after month. This accessible type of communication became a way of informing the membership of dream patterns, of inviting participation in the process of interpretation, and of encouraging attention among less aware or less interested members.

Frequently, I realized that among those who did not take an interest in the Community Dream Project were those who doubted that they had any contribution to make. So, in New Jerusalem, soon after a monthly dream night, I began approaching folks after our Sunday worship or around the neighborhood. I would approach saying, "By the way, did you have a dream last Thursday, the community dream night?" A typical reply would be, "Well, yeah, but it was kind of bizarre. Really dumb." "Please give us a copy," I'd reply, continuing, "We'd like to play with it when we go over the dreams we receive."

Once I had made just this kind of approach to Dennis M., who grinned in reply and said, "Nope. But Robin, my wife did. She said it was probably too crazy. Something about changing light bulbs in the airport." My answer was the usual one, inviting Robin to submit the dream and attend the discernment gathering. Early the next day I happened to be in the office of a friendly dreamer. "Joe," I said as I set the copier codes, "got a dream for me? Last Thursday was the community dream night, you know." "No," Joe replied, "but Carol did. She thought it was too dumb to send in. Something about changing light bulbs." I shrieked. Light bulbs again! Both dreamers brought in their dreams, each of which carried a developing theme of lay leadership. The two dreams pointed to the growing up of a community which is now adult enough to change its own light bulbs, even if our hierarchical "parents" are nervous that we'll fall and hurt ourselves. As the dream that opens this section indicates, we have grown into the confidence to take care of our own lights, which are inextricably tied into separating the old parental source of light from the new. Subsequent to the communication about the dream significance, both dreamers became more involved in the dream project. This tendency to prejudge our dreams negatively is common until we understand the language of symbol as the vehicle of spiritual communication. Such comments as the ones above would cue me to include a paragraph in the next newsletter, explaining this self-critical tendency and emphasizing the nature of the dream language as one to be learned.

Communication both among the members and between facilitator and members, becomes important in every instance of communal dreaming. Factors that affect communication include the size of the group, their commitment to the process, and the clarity of the whole organizational plan. Both in private interviews and in community meetings, members may offer their perspectives on current community issues that might be expected to appear in symbolic form. As facilitator, I am responsible for the feedback information that the dreams provide as the dream experience unfolds. For a longer term project the dreams point to next steps in the communal journey, as well as describing current issues and circumstances of the group. Sometimes the dreams are quite broad, at other times quite specific, as when a dreamer receives a curt one line dream. At a time when the New Jerusalem monthly quest had been, "How do we nourish the life that is struggling from our unconscious?" a loud clear voice was relayed to the community through one dreamer: "Do as the dreams tell you to do. Follow the instructions." (See Table 6-1 at the end of the chapter.)

Another aspect of this Community Dream Project was necessary if the community dreams were to be available to all. A Community Dream Book provided access to the entire collection of dreams. Month by month, as dreams were turned in and "played with," copies of each dream with all the comments and responses to it were placed in a large loose-leaf binder in our Center living room. *The Scroll*, the weekly bulletin, announced their placement in the book, inviting members to add their own associations to those already printed. From time to time I would collect the book, entering the new notations into my trusty computer's extensive store of information.

By the end of the formal dream research there was a total of 192 dreams in the book. It was possible to collect thirty-seven Past Dreams from members and past members who had recorded dreams during earlier years in the community. Forty dreams of my own occurred in the four months preceding the formal opening of the project. They outlined what was happening in me as organizer, as well as a plan of action, and a promise of the fulfillment of the tribal dream work. During the Community Dream Project year proper, one hundred and four dreams were collected on assigned dream nights as well as eleven labeled with their respective dates, which were received on "in-between" nights. For some time New Jerusalem continued its New Moon night agreement to attend to God's word in sleep, receiving and reporting dreams from those nights. The Sisters of Saint Joseph also created a beautifully designed dream book, with copies not only of every dream but of all material in the experiment. At Bruno, all members were provided copies of all dreams. And in the case of the Bosch family, I was able to present the mother, Marianne, and the whole family with a complete dream book record in honor of her diocesan certification as a lay minister in the Church.

An important fruit of the work has been a wider alertness to the receiving of personal as well as community dreams. A number of the adult membership at that time opted to take a six week seminar to develop greater capacity for recognizing and working with their dream symbols, and for relating this aspect of their symbolic life to the life of prayer central to religious community. As we proceed to the next chapter, attention will be given to the process step of discernment. In large groups this called for breaking groups down, and providing facilitators familiar with dream work and dream play to conduct the exploration of images.

TABLE 6-1

Monthly Dream Quests and Discerned Responses

August 31, 1989: GIVE US INSIGHT INTO THIS DREAM PROCESS AND INTO THE ONGOING LIFE OF NEW JERUSALEM.

> New Jerusalem is entering into the birth process of a new stage of her life. The dream process, too, is being "born." We must let go of the past, permitting healing of our grief and of our separation from our inner and outer authority. We are invited to wholeness.

September 29, 1989: HOW DO WE ASSIST THE BIRTH PROCESS? SHOW US HOW TO YIELD TO THE STRETCHING PAIN OF BRINGING FORTH NEW LEADERSHIP.

> Camelot is over! Trust that we are on the right track moving toward and into our renovated house, and coming from diverse directions.

October 29, 1989: WHAT IS THE FORM OF ENERGY WHICH WILL MOVE THE COMMUNITY FORWARD?

> The community must use both the masculine and feminine consciousness to put aside the fairy tale life of our beginnings and celebrate the priesthood of the people.

November 28,1989: SHOW US THE BREAKTHROUGH TO JOY!

> Celebrate your new leadership and Christ's priesthood among the people.

December 28, 1989: [Focus attention on the abundant (dream) material received in the past months. New dreams will be received and recorded from this month.]

> Learning to bring the awareness of the feminine consciousness together with the masculine continues with some struggle!

January 26, 1990: WHERE SHALL WE FIND OUR NEW LIFE, OUR NEW HOME?

> We recognize our inadequacies even as we find new life amidst a rising new consciousness and resurrection.

February 25, 1990: WE STAND ON THE EDGE OF A PRECIPICE. WHAT ARE WE TO DISCOVER IN THE DANGER?

> There is danger that what is arising from—has been born from—the unconscious will be neglected or swept back into the unconscious: i.e., Jerusalem's confidence in itself as a "holy people, a priestly nation."

March 23, 1989: [NO QUEST WAS DESIGNATED.]Differences and diversity within the community are affirmed.

April 24, 1989: HOW DO WE NOURISH THE LIFE WHICH IS STRUGGLING FROM OUR UNCONSCIOUS? WHAT PREVENTS US FROM ACCEPTING IT?
Continue the work and play of the dreams. Go fishing for them!

May 24, 1989: WE RECOGNIZE OUR CALL TO MINISTRY. SPEAK TO OUR COMMUNAL EXPRESSION OF THE CALL TO THE POOR.
Our ministry is to bring the conscious and unconscious life into relationship. To the extent that this is accomplished within the Body, it will be valid in our relationship to the poor. (A re-statement of a basic understanding of the connection between prayer and ministry.)

June 22, 1990: [EACH IS INVITED TO FORMULATE HIS/HER OWN QUESTION.]
It seems that it is a struggle for us to accept the ordinary as the place of the holy, to recognize the secular as sacred.

July 22, 1990: GIVE US DIRECTION AND WISDOM FOR OUR CHILDREN.
Three meanings of "child" appear in our dreams: a) our own children of New Jerusalem; b) the "inner child" of the community psyche; c) the "child," vulnerable and without power, represents the poor we serve. Since New Jerusalem has been formed on a theological understanding of spiritual childhood, we are to trust God's Spirit in us, recognize beauty even in our weakness, and know that, in each case above, it is the child to whom we minister.

CHAPTER SEVEN

Discernment: Getting Inside the Dream

No one person's dream, nor any one person's interpretation of a dream could validly express an entire tribal identity or the current truth of a group. There are certainly prophets among us, but any effort to define a group or to determine its future direction must be submitted to broad communal agreement.

Discernment of the dreams has developed as a key step in "unpacking" the riches of dream images. In individual dreaming, only the dream can finally affirm its own meaning, themes, and interpretation. So, in communal dreaming, the membership of the community must necessarily engage in the sense of its own history, current situation, and unique identity. This process of engagement with the symbols, of wrestling with the associations, provides members with fresh insights and sometimes astounding discoveries about their shared life.

In the New Jerusalem experiment, three women and one man joined me for monthly sifting of the New Moon dreams. It was important to have this consistent group searching out patterns and themes from one month to another. On the other hand, the discernment gatherings were always announced to the entire community, so that those who chose to join the regular discerners on any one night added depth to the exploration and understandings. The variety of communal experience often provided extended perspectives. Some persons had a facility for spotting puns, such as the "roll call" in the opening dream of Joseph's sisters. The dream, of course, dealt with the "role" of the women in the Church. Others honed in on the images of lay Christian life, or of relationship with the Church.

New Jerusalem's joyful sense of growing lay responsibility indicated a different relationship with the Church than that which appeared in the dreams of Joseph's sisters. Here the pain which women religious have suffered made itself felt in many images of anger, of deprivation, and of violence. Yet both groups, lay people and religious women, had images of priests and the priesthood of the *people*.

Among the Ursuline dreamers, lay associates joined vowed members in active contributions and discernment. The age level of discerners spanned close to fifty years, representing almost every dimension of their many ministries. As always, the meeting began with a brief presentation of basic principles. Just as in the methodology of hermeneutics—one studies a text and explores all those cultural and historical factors which underlie the shaping of it—so with the dream. Starting with the dreamer's commentary, the discerning group relates key images to the religious and communal connection, the contemporary cultural and the archetypal power of the image.

In the Ursuline experiment many present had not worked with dreams before. The participants were encouraged to trust their own perceptions of the symbolic meaning of persons, objects, and feelings within the dreams. In the first of two discerning groups, members received copies of the total dream collection beforehand, so they were quickly able to jump into the experience. This larger group was first divided into two smaller ones in order to hear from more persons and to widen the possibilities. The second gathering of nine persons had not had access to the dreams beforehand, so they first read the material silently and then worked as a single group. A playful attitude developed as the different groups discovered similar themes arising from different images.

Limitations in Community Discernment

There may surely be limitations to short term dream projects; for instance, one dream night may be helpful but what if it does not surface sufficient repetitions to identify patterns and solidify discernment? This can be overcome by having participants who continue to collect scattered dreams on the following nights. A corollary to this limitation may be a lack of time afforded to "play" with the dream symbols. Although in each case there *was* a relatively substantial number of persons present to the communal discernment of the dreams, ideally, *all* would be present to say "yes" to the description or direction that the dream symbols indicate.

Communal discernment often draws more from nonrational human events—from the instincts and feelings of qualitative analysis—than from the scientific facts of quantitative measurement. In the case of dreams, just as in sacraments, rituals and much of scripture, the language is symbolic. The symbols arise from inherent human experience, in this case that of the church community and of the life of religious believers. For profitable interpretation, dream work and dream play are necessarily synonymous if the exploration is not to slip into mere intellectual analysis. In our next chapter we raise the issue of ways to honor dreams, how to play and pray with them.

Communal Discernment

One of many synchronistic events surrounding the Community Dream Project resulted in obtaining the assistance and mentoring of Henry Reed, Ph.D. My sister, Beth, gifted with psychic powers, was unable to find direction for developing these gifts. Consequently, in 1986 she decided to register for the annual meeting of the Association for the Study of Dreams. At a seminar there she met Reed; moreover, she became a target person for the dreams of the other participants in his seminar. On the first night of the seminar everyone present incubated a dream *for* Beth. When the seminar reconvened on the next day, the patterns of the collective discernment of their dreams opened up personal life mysteries that she had long been exploring in her prayer and personal reflection. This was a life-transforming experience for Beth, one which I have since been privileged to witness in members of my own dream groups.

If groups can dream for an individual member, I thought, then why not for the group itself? I was to discover, when I contacted Reed, that he had already carried out extensive investigation along those lines. The results were extraordinary. From 1976 through 1979, Reed sponsored a theoretical community of serious dreamers throughout the country, called the Sundance Community. They were related through The Community Dream Journal, regularly communicating their dreams through it. Reed's group dreamed for the Sundance Community itself, for the United States during the Bicentennial year, and for the universe. Reed's purpose was to allow a group of very different people to experience their essential unity while providing each with a realization of a unique identity within that whole.[45]

It is in interpreting dreams that Reed has devised endless playful and refreshing applications of his theories. Haiku dream realization, The Dream Drawing Story Game, Dreaming for Others, and incubation rituals are but a few of the expressive forms of dream play which he has developed as particularly appropriate for community dream play. Personal preparation, when brought into a trusting group using these and other techniques, releases an energy that draws the group into an even more cohesive unit, and breaks through to new insights.[46]

Reed recognized the value of exploring the dreams of a community committed to common religious values. Persons who share a common spiritual vision which evolves into a particular lifestyle might be expected to access their collective unconscious more readily than others. For Christians, the ancient creed of the

Communion of Saints expresses in theological terms some of the elements Jung identifies in his religious psychology as the collective unconscious.

The first step in each discernment process has been to identify persons who could assist in planning the work and introducing it to the community membership; but, more importantly, these persons are called to sift the symbols and patterns of the dreams into pictures of significance. Mediumistic persons are often evident among those who gather regularly to share the rituals and prayer. In a group where the non-rational is respected and admired, it is easy to track down persons more than usually sensitive to the images of the psyche. In the New Jerusalem experience, therefore, I invited three women and one man to represent the membership in its function as Gatekeeper, and to become discerners. It was their role, with anyone who chose to join them, to mediate between the outer reality of our community issues and the inner reality of the dream symbols. In religious women's communities, it has been mediumistic persons who naturally rise to the occasion of encouraging the dream work, participate in the organization as well as carry out the dream work and play. In the situation of the Bosch family, it was Marianne, the mother, already deep into her dream life who served in this role.

An Example of Discerners Getting Inside the Dreams

The projects naturally fall into several areas: organizing an approach, informing the family or community, inviting participation, setting a schedule, and beginning to collect the dreams. New Jerusalem wanted to connect their dream work to some flow of nature, remembering with some regret the loss of such rhythmic Catholic celebrations as Rogation Days. Since fasting and feasting welcomed the change of seasons, processions, prayers for planting, or blessings of the harvest became natural expressions of union with nature. Thus the community chose the night of the New Moon symbolizing creativity and new birth. The next step to be taken was discernment.

Our coming together was quite homey—more gathering than meeting. I check out the living room of our community Pastoral Center or welcome the group to my own home. Water on the kitchen stove, there follows the setting up of a newsprint pad and the placing of our dream candle in the center of a large low table. Barb arrives, her package usually promising a set of pictures. Her straightforward dreams and clear imagery flow smoothly into gentle watercolors to be displayed at our Sunday worship gathering. Then Joe slides in, grinning, his slow drawl happily easing our pace. Mary and Kathleen may come excited about their preparation, appreciating pre-meeting copies of the dreams. We welcome other community members who have opted to join us, especially as they strengthen our own enthusiasm for the Dream Project and its ongoing effect on community life. Usually dreams of visiting discerners have been included among those submitted from the membership.

Coffee and tea collected from the kitchen, we settle into moments of silence and inner listening. At a natural moment we begin to look at the first dream, asking *where is the community meaning in this story?* Our papers have already been marked with associations, possibilities, and reactive emotions. The newsprint has been prepared, with words or phrases listed to identify key images. The dreamers call out associations, which are then listed, until we instinctively pause to review what has been recorded. Each person, armed with magic marker, is free to step up to the easel, drawing lines of connection, voicing new associations, recognizing themes of our current life together.

Puzzles arise. We settle back and "wander" around the images. I share responses from previously taped interviews among random members. We pass around a sketch that a dreamer has included with his notes. Reconsidering an understanding, we realize a whole new theme is appearing in several dreams. There may be a gasp of amazement when Barb reads a late submitted dream and remembers an almost identical one of her own a few nights before. Paying attention, we ask, "What is this saying?" I encourage the dreamers to bring their own drawings. One person agrees to call Joann, whose notation says that her dream would make a good Far Side cartoon. An active hour and a half passes by as too short a time. Then the group reviews themes, aware of patterns from earlier months. Finally quiet settles as we look at the monthly posted question to which the dreams are a response.

The "posted question" (See Table 6-1) represents our Dream Quest, the term for the monthly articulation of our desire to hear God's word through dreams. When we place a new quest before God, it is as if it unfolds from the dream work we have just completed. It leads us into future dreaming. The atmosphere shifts as someone lights the dream candle. Gathered now in silence, there is an air of satisfaction with the work just completed. These are the community discerners about to identify the dream issue for the next month. Waiting. Listening. Joe steps forward and places his community symbol, the New Jerusalem cross, on the table near the candle. He suggests his wording of the quest for which the community will dream. Soon another places a commitment form on the table. A small painting follows, then a picture of our founder. With each statement that accompanies placement of a personal symbol, the issue becomes clearer. Soon all nod in consensus. Yes, this is what we ask God to speak to on our next dream night! There is anticipation as the mugs are returned to the kitchen, the easel folded, the room straightened, and the candle snuffed. What will the Spirit show us this month as we continue opening ourselves to our dreams, seeking God's word, and acting on that word?

The Community as Gatekeeper

I am at the entrance to a passageway that leads downward—somewhat like an escalator. I realize that I am a gatekeeper, and I must check to see that whoever enters takes nothing with them. An old woman descends past me. She needs to take some things with her. I help her by quickly giving her precious stones, gold and silver chains, and some salts. I place them on her tray which is like one half of a scale. She moves down to a grassy area below, hangs the stones from the chains and sprinkles the salt on the ground in a rectangular pattern. I, the gate-keeper, move down and to the right to a position where I can better see what she is doing.

Like a tour guide, I explain to my observing self and to Gary and John what the woman is doing. And I describe the various ways that different cultures have of worshipping using the right brain. I stress how important it is when a people or culture don't use the right brain or the non-verbal, isolated persons must serve that function for the society and are often seen as "crazies" (NJ Dream 8.083189 - <u>The Gatekeeper,</u> Mary G.A.).

The image of Gatekeeper has appeared twice in community dreams. In this case the dreamer, Mary, has ministered for a number of years as the person who welcomed and prepared initiates for membership in New Jerusalem Community. In the role of Gatekeeper she represents the membership, standing between the inner life of the community's collective unconscious and the outer life of conscious choice and action. Acting much as the ego does for each individual person, the Gatekeeper, the membership, decides what may move freely into the community's memory, its prayer, what will shape its inner life. What enters there may not be the fruits of the ego, but only the Wisdom of the community's experience, represented by the old woman.

Does the Gatekeeper also decide what comes forth from the unconscious? The dream itself does not reveal a direct answer to this question, but there is no indication that she *prevents* this movement outward. The membership's willing reflection on its dreams, its inner resource of faith and prayer, its supply of symbols, may supposedly come forth freely to take conscious action in the reality of daily living and in responsibility for shaping a more just world. Jeremy Taylor devotes an early chapter of his book on dreams to the relationship between dream work and social responsibility, stating:

> [Dream] work strengthens the commitment and resolve to change, both collectively and personally. It overcomes the inevitable depression . . . that overtakes those engaged in attempting to promote change in a society that fears and resists [it].[47]

Consideration of Mary's dream highlights more than the image of the gate-keeper, who acts as both teacher and tour guide. As is usual with dreams, there is meaning to each detail. Working with each image will serve to illustrate our manner of interpreting and playing with any of our dreams. Those familiar with dream work will recognize quickly the archetypal nature of the images; however, our direct references to Jung's archetypal interpretation always *followed* our first spontaneous responses. We related the symbols first within our Christian context and New Jerusalem's specific life history. Often as not, the archetypal perspective only confirmed the "truth" we had arrived at; at other times, when we were puzzled or uncertain, it broke open a fresh or astonishing revelation.

The passage downward is the passage into the community's collective unconscious, moving smoothly like an escalator. Although the gatekeeper is to let no one take anything "down" with them, she makes no objection to the old woman. In fact, she assists this figure of the community's wisdom who asks no permission, has no doubts about her right to enter the unconscious. She is wise because she is confident of her life experience. It is her task to take the precious treasures of hard won integration into the deepest center of the community's identity.

The precious stones and salt are both crystalline forms representing wholeness; however, the beauty of the stones is not because they are translucent. Rather, stones have imperfections which create their own kind of opaque beauty, an expression of the mystery of our human weakness, which Saint Paul declares is its strength.[48] Jung's research into alchemy indicates that human myths are replete with images of the stone as the symbol of the self.[49] The salt, however, is pure crystal. Gold and silver in mythology, alchemy, and other symbolic systems represent the most divine in human nature, and in this particular parallelism both the masculine gold and feminine silver dimensions of divinity are represented.

The discerners see in the symbol of the tray, which is one half of a scale, a telling reference to an ongoing community issue. Always a dynamic tension exists between the call to the contemplative—the inner dimension of the Christian experience—and the active urge to respond to the outer human needs of the world. The "Wisdom" figure of the dream experiences no such difficulty. She knows justice must necessarily be granted to the inner life, also, as placing the symbols of community wholeness on the tray indicates. The balance of justice requires that one half of the scale reside in the inner world, providing the groundedness upon which the work of justice in the outer world can depend.

The grassy area indicates a place of rest and growth. The salt is scattered in a rectangular pattern to indicate, again, completeness. The four-sided figure is an ancient one, reminiscent of many dreams in which the theme of four directions is repeated, as well as its symbolism for the City, Jerusalem.[50] The "membership" moves down and to the right to see what "wisdom" is doing.

Many of us are familiar with recent studies of the right and left brain functions: the right brain controls creative, intuitive functions, and the left brain controls functions of logic and objectivity. Here the emphasis is on the right brain which in our analytic world is often judged as foolish and useless. It is this mysterious and significant world of dream symbol that is deemed useless and even narcissistic. It is only fair to report that the dream work itself raised questions of utility and of meaning among some community members. It seems so "crazy," so unrelated to the desperate and urgent struggles of humanity.

The Gatekeeper, the community membership, follows the wisdom figure, watches her, explains to herself and two participating masculine figures what Wisdom is doing. Gary W. and John Q. are valued former members who originally were instrumental in shaping the inner life of prayer and worship; furthermore, both, in their time among us, unashamedly shared the ways in which their personal dreams opened up God's word to them. In other dreams Gary as Jesuit and John as Franciscan appear as head and heart. They remain in our friendship and consciousness as those who minister the fruits of the *inner* reality by the active priestly work of their *outer* reality in larger global arenas.

NJ Dream 86 shares a related image of a gatekeeper who, as in Mary's dream, is central to an action that involves an inner-outer movement. In this, also, a jewel appears, shaped almost identically to the New Jerusalem logo.

> *The Gatekeeper, a woman, seems to be at the center of the meaning and of the geography of the setting. I am moving toward her. I am encouraged by the tribe as I go. We are in the atmosphere of Indian country. There are Indians and Hispanics in and around a truck. There are quiet beatings and drumming. I am still at a distance from the gatekeeper who is wearing a lovely jeweled pendant* (NJ Dream 86.052490 - The Indian Connection, Pat B.).

Anyone in every tribe is invited to join discernment gatherings that follow the collection of dreams. In a family or small community, the members are much more likely to rub elbows daily, providing informal moments to remember, laugh and converse about the dreams. In larger groups, various members may come at scattered times. In this case, a core group must provide continuity and center the discussion, just as fresh members enrich the association work with their perspectives. As if a metaphor for community itself, the individual contribution strengthens, complements and colors the interpretation of the communal dreams. Drawing very large groups into the discernment process presents special challenges and certain advantages. In this latter case, small groups can be set to work and play with specific dreams. Or newsprint with dreams and images can be posted around a large room with participants able to wander among them, making notations, discussing among themselves, listing endless possibilities. The advantage in designing such strategies is that everyone can give input. Still, a final group must collect and collate these responses.

Patterns and Themes

The records of the dream projects suggest that different archetypal themes arise within each community. As archetypes, themes such as the masculine and feminine, are coming to such consciousness in many cultures that it would be surprising *not* to find its symbols in almost every community's collection of dreams. Pioneer images, however, such as we saw in the Bruno community's dreams, may be archetypal but may not apply everywhere; in fact, it is the *city* which appears often in the New Jerusalem collection, affirming the group's call to an integrated working class neighborhood.

Themes tend to be tightly woven into the fiber of the communal life as lived experience. In that sense, it is difficult to separate them from one another. The overlapping is natural and strengthens the whole garment. Selecting those that are most cogent provides central connections to the others. Without exception, the themes are to be understood in the context of the tribal story. Currents flowing through the collective life arise in the dreams, sometimes astounding the dream discerners, often consoling them. The expectation that the Spirit of God dwelling among the people will be revealed through a dream venture or common quest seems to be met. Jung had said:

> Dreams are impartial, spontaneous products of the unconscious psyche, outside of the control of the will. They are pure nature; they show us the unvarnished natural truth (CW, v. 10, *Civilization in Transition*, "The Meaning of Psychology for Modern Man," 149).

Knowing that the dream is a symbol over which the "ego" has little or no control, members receive a dream with increasing awe and awareness that its source is from deep within their own psyches, as well as from a Mystery greater than their collective union in community.

Conclusion

The process of tracking and interpreting the dream has been one of discernment. As Christians committed to listening to the God within, we have been delighted, and often startled, at the specificity of the dream images. The discernment process is an ancient ascetical practice of the Christian community, used to sift the spirits of darkness from the spirits of light in terms of the most hidden human desires and the nature of its impulses. It involves attention to subjective as well as objective material in distinguishing what is valuable and what is hazardous in the spiritual journey. It was Ignatius of Loyola, founder of the Society of Jesus, who first studied the long history of mystical experience, as well as his own experience; then, he formulated systematic forms—personal and communal—for ascertaining the will of God by this method. Contemporary humanistic psychology is rediscovering this method of qualitative exploration under the heading of hermeneutics and heuristics. Both the text of the dream, and its subjective effects on the community as dreamer, have provided meaning that describes a new level of community identity.

It is by these methods that the dream discerners bring together their own associations with the communal connection to particular symbols. Archetypal information is considered. Dreams are promulgated and spontaneous responses from other members are recorded. Informal interviews expand the store of reaction and questioning among members. As discerners meet, the gathered dreams begin to cluster into themes which call for greater focus.

In describing the experiments and discernment of each tribe, we have made note of their particular themes. New Jerusalem was moving from a crisis period to one of new life. All of the Ursuline themes focused on what is truly central to their present development, the transition which is taking place in religious life. For Joseph's Sisters the place of women in the Church related to or even permeated most of their themes. For the Bosch family the dream project itself was experienced as a source of transformation. In each case, the theme was shaped out of a cluster of dreams dealing with the same images or meaning.

It is inviting to take these patterns of fascination and intrigue into further investigation through methods of right-brain play. In this way the community may unravel a hidden meaning or heighten its awareness of the dream message as God's word. Next we will consider the role of play, rituals and worship in honoring dreams as another way of expressing God's word.

CHAPTER EIGHT

Honoring the Dreams

In these past chapters dreamers have walked a new and, for many, a strange road. They have confronted their dreams, welcomed their apparent idiosyncrasies, conversed with them, and given them a place in their communal psyche. This relationship is not yet complete, however, until the dreamers honor the messages the dreams offer and celebrate their significance. Why are they to do this?

The dreams have yielded much of what is needed to connect inner reality with outer reality. Now the dreamers must cooperate by taking action, by bringing the message to some measure of fulfillment. It is not the need of the dream itself, but the need of every human, to express the God-experience, which occurs at the heart of the Self-experience. By projecting the experience out into the fresh air of consciousness, one is further enlightened and the experience itself can blossom. Thus, consonant with all of this work, the *community* needs to express the inner experience of the group in the objective world of consciousness. Two basic approaches by which this is accomplished appear in many variations in the midst of the developing dream process.

One approach may appear immediate and obvious, although the "how to" may not be as clear or available at first glance. The approach is simply for the dreamers to change their behavior. Perhaps better said, they need to permit the transformation implied in the dream to take full possession of them. Sometimes awareness itself is enough to permit this to happen, whereas at other times members of the group must commit themselves to take action on the content of their lives to which the dreams point. A good example lies in the series of dreams Richard Rohr had between 1982 and 1984. They led him away from the New Jerusalem community in 1985.

> *I am walking east of the monastery, . . . It gets darker and darker. . . . I have let both my (masculine and feminine) unconscious die* (NJ Past Dream 000082 - The Most Beautiful Part of the Monastery, Richard R.).

> *A long series of war images and feelings. . . . Sad, pathetic, scary. . . . Sense of tragedy and inevitability calling forth more compassion than anger. My heart is very soft, even if trapped* (NJ Past Dream, Slow Motion War, Richard R.).

> *I am in the family home. . . . My Father is the only other person (there). It is cleaned out but we are not going to move (yet). I decide to destroy the house by flooding it from within. . . . I then tell Daddy what I'm going to do with some trepidation. He very gently tells me that I should not do that. It would ruin the house* (NJ Past Dream, Flooding the House, Richard R.).

> *The vestments I am wearing are too many, too heavy, but so special that I don't want to take them off even though they are holding me back from getting to the church. . . . I am aware that I am losing my breath, . . . even if I get there, I will not be peaceful and the (homily) will not come from my truthful self.*
> *I feel I am hiding from the aimed guns of an enemy and from eyes that are everywhere and all-seeing* (NJ Past Dream, Commissioned to the Ecumenical Council, Richard R.).

The archetypal father is so identified with his community that these dreams are easily understood as personal dreams as well as the exposition of the communal soul. The call to a more contemplative pace of life causes more than tension. A war breaks out within Richard, caught as he is between his responsibility to the community and his real desire to make a radical change that would free him from the many heavy roles with which he is burdened. The war is expressed in the *community* as members take sides for and against Richard's plans, feeling rejected by him and casting their own missives. To be truthful to himself becomes increasingly central to Richard, and he moves ahead with plans, takes action, goes through closure processes, and moves on.

The community floods Richard with needs, desires to be a part of his move, criticisms of his feelings. The "aimed guns of the enemy" were within his own house. The war continues for some time on both sides, but later peters out as the fruits of the change become evident for *both* Richard and for the community.

Richard's life, though busy, becomes more focused and simplified. The community takes on the responsibility for its own life and leadership. Acting clearly on the messages of the dream, changing behaviors and lifestyle serves both the personal dreamer and the community as it honors the dream.

Often enough, however, even after association with the images, symbols are only *partially* revealed in their significance. The emerging message is unclear or incomplete. In this case, taking direct action is not appropriate. How can the dreamers access what cannot be forced? Although association of images with the communal experience is a pressing first step, the community or family may not catch a scattered meaning or may not be gripped enough by an image to act on or to celebrate its meager and incomplete existence. If it is not yet clear *how* behaviors or attitudes are to be changed, the dreamers must bring it to life by honoring it in another way. Some of these ways are described in the next section.

To Play and To Pray

As inhibition surrenders to the causes of honoring, celebrating, and coming to new insights, "playing and praying" come to an essential oneness. Not unlike contemplation, union of the interior spirit with the expression of action can be an almost ecstatic new experience of the God-life. Perhaps few dream researchers have brought such playfulness to the intensity of dream "work" as Henry Reed, often called the "father of the modern dream work movement." [51]

Reed has the capacity to invite the dreamer into delightful and uncomplicated ways of preparing the psyche for dreaming, as well as for extending and celebrating the inner mystery. Twenty-five or more years before the current flood of dream publications, Reed led his students in creating dream pillows and shields, in ongoing conversations with dream characters, in unique meditative stances. He entices the hesitant participant to express the dream experience. It is his transpersonal dreamwork that planted yet another seed of the tribal dream concept.

In an overnight healing service, Reed invites one person to be the target of the others' dreams. S/he may well find him or herself with a gathering of strangers. After appropriate dream incubation within the group, and a group ritual in which the target person shares simple possessions with the others, all retire to receive a *dream for that person.* The morning gathering is pregnant with excitement as each shares the gift of a dream for the chosen person. Having used this method in seminars and retreats, I can testify to the extraordinary synchronicity among the dreams and their revelatory impact on the dreamer. This research of Henry Reed's opened the question for me: If a group can dream for *one* person, why not for a *group* of persons, a community? With Reed, these were not just experiments, but developed ceremonies for bringing dreams to vital awareness and effective life changes for dreamers.

A Spring Symbol Celebration

The Spring Symbol Celebration at New Jerusalem expanded celebration of communal dream symbols by letting its members get into the guts and hearts of other images that had arisen over the years from prayer, communal practice, and other fruits of the unconscious. The Spring Symbol Celebration, a Saturday carnival of symbols, not only marked the end of a long dull winter, but also opened up play with the meaning of community symbols other than dreams. Using its key scriptural image, that of the Holy City, the New Jerusalem, a generous group of friends helped in setting up Twelve "Gates," each of which represented a major community symbol or dream image. At each Gate, one type of symbol was played out in order to touch on its mystery and its revelation.

Introduced by a map presented at the entrance, eleven "Gates of the City" provided options where a unique event was occurring at each. The Twelfth Gate of the City was reserved for an evening session where enactment of a major dream, "Are You the One Who is to Come?" would lead us first to "prison," then to the "ballroom" of our freedom (NJ Other 120289).

At one Gate, a banner was being reconstructed citing the community founding prophecy. At another, personal symbols were being made. In another space a circle dance culminated at the Tree of Life, where each dancer was mounting his/her symbol. We mixed and baked the normality of life into the breads for our evening party. The smell of rising dough at the Body of Christ Symbol Gate and the drums reverberating from the Boiler Room brought together the community's most domestic and primitive selves, the complementarity and the chaos of our feminine and masculine consciousness. Game boards were devised from the directions that appeared in dreams. At the Gate representing our Call to the Poor, members were provided with paper and stamped envelopes, invited to write their Congress persons about social issues which concerned them.

The evening closure, Gate 12, drew others who had not been a part of the afternoon experience. With her usual humor and lightness of spirit, Barb G. led us through the dream. We walked in solemn procession through the yard of our "prison," heard the whispered word of hope, met one another's glance, and broke into dancing and singing as we were "liberated" (NJ Other 120289). Brothers and sisters who had not "hung out" together through the long winter, devoured bread and "champagne" together. Then we sat down to break open our personal experience of the dream enactment. At one point in this sharing, Mary Frances turned to me and asked how I felt, if I was disappointed that the numbers were smaller than I had hoped for. The very asking of the question raised clarity about my feelings. The day itself had been filled with play. Those who *had* joined in the event and those who attended had a real moment of being bonded. As I had observed folks taking time to talk and share I saw their contentment, and felt my own quiet joy through the day. We were community for those who were not present there with us. We were laughing and celebrating and giving ourselves to one another. There was warmth and new vitality among us. The community understood anew what it meant to be "re-membered" into our community Body.

The Spring Symbol Celebration was complete and had become a vital experience for those who came to play and those who came to work. (All the same in a symbol experience!) This elaborate celebration truly honored the many expressions of our tribal symbol life. The Tree of Life created that day is now in the communal Upper Room where it is collecting more symbols as time goes on. The weaving, which hangs in the community Center hallway, grows and becomes more colorful as threads and ribbons and strings are added.

In each case, the community is invited to explore the mystery of the symbol. The membership asks, "If a particular symbol did *once* influence the tribe, how does it *now* affect us or move us to action? Is the symbol still 'alive' among us?" Thomas Merton has said that symbolism opens the way to an intuitive understanding of mystery, and it places us in the presence of the invisible. It seem that the symbol, like the Gatekeeper of Chapter Seven, leads the membership down into that underground place of their lives. There God of wisdom and balance reigns. As we confront darkness and terror, bringing them to the light of consciousness, God leads us to embrace the mystery and live it out.

Some Areas of Expression for Communal Dreams

The following categories outline a number of possible ways to honor the dream. We have already explored, in Chapter Five, the power of names to express a community's identity. Let us now inquire into other expressions for honoring a dream symbol or other communal image. Samples from our research communities suggest ways by which the dream might be expressed. Its very expression frequently gives new perception and energy to the group.

❖ NATURE IMAGES - Experiences of nature are surely the most basic in human life. Perduring groups of indigenous and primitive tribes have remained close to and dependent on nature's providence. Yet even persons living in highly cultivated societies must return to nature for rest, renewal and the ultimate provision of needs. Not surprisingly, then, a wide span of seasonal images pervades the overall collection of tribal dreams: weather patterns, roving animals, or journey images through various landscape settings, and many more.

> *I am living in the city on a busy corner. Many people are walking on the sidewalk and getting off a crowded bus. The house is not visible, but a patch of yard has sturdy young trees glazed over with ice. The soil is rich, the trees are beautiful. How beautiful they will be when Spring comes* (SSJ 3, 031993 - Good Soil, Helen B.).

In the discernment meeting the sisters knew their own tribal psyche in this description. In the midst of busyness, pressures, and demands, their communal life seems to be frozen over. But the life itself is sturdy. They believe, without exception, that spring is coming, the ice will melt. The soil of spirituality and of the Church is rich and new leaves will surely sprout. The sisters walked and danced throughout this dream. Another way by which the community could have honored the dream, would have been to plant a tree as a promise of the new life to come.

In the dream, quoted in Chapter Two (SSJ 1, 31993, The Plunge, Mary Rita S.), water is the ready image to be employed in honoring the dream itself. Celebrations such as camping trips, hiking, river rafting, or visits to native American habitats would all be ways to honor the meaning of this dream. It reminds me of a group who took a cross-country bicycle trip to celebrate a community anniversary. Plunging into such an adventure demonstrates openness to what the road ahead will provide in the way of filling or challenging one's basic needs for food, rest, and safety.

❖ BODY AS SYMBOL - Readers of the New Testament have a strong metaphor for the human body in Saint Paul's famous Letter to the Corinthians (I Cor. 12:12-31). It presents a message of unity and differences. We are embodied persons, so the familiar incarnation "in which we live and move and have our being" sends constant messages that touch into the body's reality and into the deeper lessons the body can teach us.

In an upstairs room there is a woman who has had surgery or been in an accident . . . she is speaking as if with an electronic voice-box on her chest—the archetype of the rejected or socially avoided person, unloved. So, with some sense of compassion, I approach her. She reaches out and begins to touch me—then she is touching me all over, with "desperate affection"—but this seems to be healing— her voice suddenly becomes natural and returns to her throat. Her face emerges from the shadows, almost as if she had been kept in a cupboard and she now looks perfectly normal (NJ Past Dream 041788 - The Unloved Woman Transformed, Gary W.).

What kind of reflections might a community make on this graphic dream? What is it saying about its tribal soul? The voice of the feminine is named here as the area for transformation through healing. If the group already recognizes the nature of its unloved feminine, they might prepare a forum for women's voices to be heard relative to a particular need or issue in the community. However, as ritual, the expression of the "deformity" being healed would certainly call for physical gestures that are a respectful honoring of the body of the "woman." The dream suggests that the gift of "touch" is the cure. This is an obvious opportunity to create ritual for the community's healing, a blessing with oil or laying of hands on one another. Such blessings and anointing rituals are common in most religious groups, and this dream encourages the integration of this kind of prayer with the acknowledgement of the feminine deformity or loss unique to this group. The communal prayer would be designed not just to bring the feminine out of the shadows, but to provide for her continuance in the light.

❖Rites and Ceremonies - It is to be expected in Catholic communities—where word and gesture are inherent to every faith moment—that rites and ceremonies will highlight almost any kind of celebration, most forms of prayer, or the most ordinary community events. For our purposes of honoring a dream, simple prayer rites or ceremonies extend the dream's meaning and heighten its affective power.

New Jerusalem found that treating a scripture passage as a *great dream belonging to all of humanity*, yielded a moving ritual of healing. A teenager in the community had been diagnosed with a serious mental illness. Her suffering had been prolonged painfully over several years, so she welcomed her parents' suggestion that her church community gather to pray for her. Her father and a supportive friend led the ceremony with the following passage:

In Jerusalem there is a pool with five porticoes; its Hebrew name is Bethesda. The place is crowded with sick people—those who are blind, lame or paralyzed—lying there waiting for the water to move. An angel of God comes down to the pool from time to time to stir up the water; the first one to step into the water after it has been stirred up is completely healed.

One person had been there for thirty-eight years. Jesus, who knows this person has been sick a long time, says, "Do you want to be healed?"

"Rabbi," the sick one answers, "I don't have anyone to put me into the pool. . . . By the time I get there, someone else has gone in ahead of me." Jesus replies, "Stand up! Pick up your mat and walk." The individual is immediately healed, picks up the mat and walks away (John 5:1-9).[52]

It happens that the downstairs worship space can only be reached by a ramp or two sets of steps, all of which move downward into the wide room. In this setting, one can well imagine the descent into a pool of water.

A very large bowl of water centered the room with scattered small cards with the names of angels on them at its base. Chairs were arranged in a complete circle around it. After introductory remarks and the reading of the gospel "dream," the leaders invited those gathered to come forward and choose an angel card. The cards offered "Patience," "Obedience," "Joy," or a myriad of other angelic companions. Those engaged in the healing prayers were encouraged to use the name of their angel as a direction of prayer for this younger sister of theirs and as a spiritual discipline. During an extended time of song and prayer, one by one members came forward and "stirred the waters," articulating aloud or in the silence of their hearts, a loving prayer for the sick girl. Creating a ceremony directly from scripture is almost identical to same process for honoring a dream, and brings the blessing of God's word into immediate contact with the community's need. With great love and support of friends and family, this young woman has now faced and is dealing with the complications of her illness.

❖ ART AND ITS FORMS - With almost every experiment, art was employed in a way that unfolded meaning or triggered transformation. Quilts, banners, weavings, as well as haikus and other forms of poetry were drawn upon from the countless forms of art that can be called on to express the inner experience.

Drawings and mandalas were used frequently, as in the case of the Way of Life group's reflective evening exercise. Each of the six members shared a sense of her mandala without analysis. The next morning, a dream enlightened what had been unrecognized the night before: an umbilical cord now clearly seen in one mandala. In exploring alternative ways to live professional religious life, holding onto the cord that carries the source of life will nourish and steady religious communities in the midst of what could be runaway changes.

Shields and masks are alternate mandala forms. Animal or human face masks express the soul of the tribe or community. The mask may be suggested by a dream, or, often, by a particular quality of the group's character. When a shaman dons an eagle mask, for instance, s/he *is* an eagle. When a family makes face masks together, any one of these masks will be an expression of more than that one person in the family. It will in some way reveal the whole family.

Quilting is another art practiced throughout the world. The making of a community quilt is more than a dialog between one artist and a one medium, however. The skills of this art function to bring a number of folks together. It is an opportunity to gather, to tell stories, to laugh and to enjoy one another. The energy of many hands, shared work, and the art of visiting are all combined in the quilting bee. In church communities, quilters may make a quilt for a member whose life is being celebrated in a special way, or for a raffle. The work may be applied, also, to mark an important event in the community's history. So quilters are frequently found in such communal groups.

❖ MINISTRY AND SERVICE - A dreamer had the following dream as her community was preparing to join a March for the Homeless in Washington, D.C. The march, indeed, was a way to honor the dream; moreover, the dream points to the total ministerial commitment of the community. The dream could also have been acknowledged by an evangelizing trip, or the commissioning of persons being trained for service. In New Jerusalem, it was one of many birth dreams in the re-birthing period recorded during the dream project year.

The dream opens like [the movie] <u>Brother Sun, Sister Moon</u>, a lovely field of flowers in the sunlight. A man, a Saint Francis figure in a robe, strides across the field, self-assured, calm. He comes giving peace and confidence.

The scene shifts and the man is lying on a pallet in a simple barn . . . with straw. The man's body is shifting and twisting and I realize that this man is about to give birth. His legs are open and his robe is above his knees.

He is in the throes of labor . . . from his legs come forth little Saint Francis figures. They are animated, dancing, each one coming forth carrying a cross, . . . Not in despair and burden, but with each cross a commission. There are so many that the line stretches out, and they joyfully carry their crosses on the way (NJ Other Dream, 102989 - The Francis In Us, Sue C.).

❖ IMAGES UNIQUE TO A TRIBE—There are times when the dream speaks very directly to the practice or life habits of a particular tribe. The group realizes with astonishment and wonder how truly the symbol is directed to *their* collective psyche. In the case of Catholic religious orders, whose history is often measured in hundreds of years, the dream may pull the tribe into its primary mythic level.

This happened with the Bruno Ursulines whose "pioneer schoolhouse" dream of Chapter Three does not stop at the level of the sisters' more recent early century history, but moves deeper. The sixteenth century birth of the community, in the founding vision of Angela Merici, is depicted as a ladder leading to the heavens. The reference is not disconnected from the image of lights that cannot be put out: Angela had prophesied that her Company of women would continue until the end of time.

❖ ENACTING THE DREAM AS RITUAL CELEBRATION - Enactment of a dream that functions as a communal parable often precipitates excitement and fun. And this may further trigger a transformation of perception into action. Dream enactment was used in the Ursuline Convocation workshop, providing a closure ritual that was both lively fun and inspiring prayer. The workshop concluded somewhat spontaneously and playfully with a ritual employing this dream.

I am in a church full of people held by Satan, in darkness. . . . After a time I throw in a . . . big glass of water.

Then I am in a pew and a procession of children come in. I take the program I have or the bulletin of several pages and hold it out to catch fire from the candles. This is what we need to burn up all the Evil. Lots of people hold these out. There is chaos and fighting to reclaim the Church and—I carry my torch over the communion rail and into the sanctuary as I fight (UBC, Saving the Church, Lucy S).

The dream presents an archetypal struggle between good and evil taking place in a church setting. The group chose to honor the dream by first becoming a procession of children offering lighted candles from which to set fire to their (rational) "programs." The workshop participants enacting the dream carried their torches in the midst of chaos and fighting, and reclaimed the Church by leaping over the communion rail into the sanctuary. It was with great glee that they permitted themselves to be enlightened by the inner child of their Ursuline life, enabling them to let go of the constant analysis of current religious life. Can the reader imagine the myriad meanings for religious women as the group "carried the torch," overcame the division between the ordained and non-ordained which the paradoxical term "communion rail" images, and entered the holy of holies?

Such occasions provide ideal times to enact dreams of the community. The effect is often the same when a dreamer plays with a personal dream by drawing it, dancing it, or simply discussing it with another. Awareness is heightened. There is an "Aha!" experience. A flash of understanding seldom stands alone, but frequently is accompanied by a rush of emotional recognition and response. Although taking action on a dream may assume a more pragmatic form, such as changing a long term habit or initiating a new work, this playful approach widens the mystery of our tribal images as had occurred in the Spring Symbol Celebration.

Using Dream Closure Rituals

As completion of long-term dream projects, enactment celebrations have served several groups to coalesce feelings of joyful release and satisfaction with their dream work. These celebrations have acted as "summaries" of dream discernment. The following dream took life as Joseph's sisters concluded their Chapter work. The dream had arrived *before* the agreed upon dream date, and after the dreamer had been talking to a friend about congregational dreams. There are clearly named characters in this drama, describing multiple persons in the communal psyche, and a ready collection of symbols for summarizing their current situation. When the Chapter completed its theological reflection and had drawn up directional statements, the one hundred and fifty members were invited to follow a dreamer's rendition of her dream by casting themselves into one of the dream roles.

> I am in a large old church. The walls are stone, but the lower half is covered with dark wood, like mahogany, and is quite ornate. I go to the choir loft. I can see that the church is a little over half full. The people are seated throughout the church with empty spaces around them.
>
> In the choir loft the organist begins to talk to me. He tells me how important it is to him and especially the pastor to have the church filled with music during Mass. If he plays the organ softly, the people don't sing, and if he plays loud, he will drown out any singing that people do. He is very distraught, and doesn't know how to get the people to sing. It is very important that they sing. I empathize with him and decide to go downstairs and sing the best I can and hope that will encourage others around me.
>
> I go downstairs and toward the front of the church. There is an alcove off the side and in this alcove is a large gathering of Sisters of Saint Joseph. Mass has started, and the group of SSJs are talking softly to each other. They do not say much, but there is a lot of communication taking place. I tell them about the

organist and the concern about the music. The priest (pastor at the church I am at, Fr. X) reads the gospel. It is short. He then tells the congregation how tired he is. There was a big parish social the night before and several meetings he had to attend. He is just exhausted. He tells the people that he is just too tired to preach, and that we would just have some quiet time for reflection. He sits down. He looks so exhausted. I wonder if he will be able to finish Mass.

When he stands for the intercessions, I start to leave the alcove and so do all the SSJs. I am in the middle of the group. It is as if an unspoken communication went through the group and everyone agreed to join the congregation and help with the singing.

As we go into the body of the church, we fill in the empty spaces. As I come to a pew with an empty space on the end, I start to slip into the pew and the woman who is already in the pew tells me she will leave and sit someplace else so I can be with my friends. I tell her to please not move. We do not want to displace anyone. She chose this seat and should keep it. It is her seat. WE JUST WANT TO FILL IN WHERE THERE ISN'T ANYONE. She appreciates this, and is glad we are joining the congregation but not moving anyone out.

When the offertory hymn starts, the singing is just a little louder than before with our extra voices, but people seem surprised to hear others singing. I can see some of them pulling out hymn books and starting to join us. The singing continues to grow in volume until the whole church is filled with music.

As the singing swells, everyone joins in more enthusiastically. I can feel the vibration of the music. It is a wonderful, joyous feeling. Everyone in the church is looking at each other and smiling. There is a feeling that together we have done a great thing (SSJ 53, 030994 - <u>Sing A New Song</u>, Emily S.).

Let us look at this great "drama" and meet the major characters. First you will meet *the people* scattered throughout the church. It is half empty. One lay person among them will eventually protest their sense of being "in the way of" the sisters. *The organist* becomes the source of a call to action. He is distraught at the lack of participation. The singing is poor. *A group of sisters* is standing off to the side, uninvolved, but communicating and open to leadership from the "I", or membership. Enter *the exhausted priest*. He names the cause of his deep weariness, announces that he can't preach and sits down. *The protesting woman* is the apologetic aspect of the soul, which is put at ease by a sister, now acting out an evolving transformation. (*The transformation* itself, and *the song* that grows voluminously are also, in a sense, "characters" in this drama.) Leading us through the dream is the original dreamer, identified by the "I", and representing the communal membership. Groups of twenty to thirty persons take on the enactment of each role.

The People

The place of this enactment by the Chapter body is the large community chapel. A space is created in the center with chairs and a few sisters scattered as "the lay people."

110

The Organist

A group of about thirty sisters offers to take the role of the distraught organist. As the dreamer reads this section, they wave frantically at the people attempting to get them to sing, they slap their foreheads in frustration and wipe their brows. They shake their heads in disappointment. (Perhaps the intensity of their desperation is heightened by their reality as past or present teachers and liturgists!) A thin wavering song begins to be heard.

A Group of Sisters

As the sample theme statement in Chapter Two (p. 33) describes, many Joseph's sisters' dreams pointed to a community tendency to sit back, to take an observing position, or to be off to the side of events. The "I" of the dream moves among this group, *encouraging them to sing their song*, affirming the community and urging them to enter into the center of the Church. A few other voices join the effort.

The Exhausted Priest

The large group that undertakes this role brought much laughter from the total assembly. They recognized and could express their own total ministerial exhaustion. They were doubtless aware of the constant task forces and committees, and the extracurricular work that accompanies ministerial service. Here the group staggered a bit and hung their arms from the shoulders to the knees. Shaking their heads in a "I-can't-do-it anymore" mode, they lowered themselves—exhausted— into their chairs.

The Protesting Woman

The song is not yet so loud that we cannot hear the apologetic tone of the protesting lay woman, or the firm response of the "Congregation." The group carrying the role of the lay woman starts to rise, then settles back in its place. This key moment expresses an original understanding of the founding women of the Sisters of Saint Joseph. They are called to "fill in" where no one else is serving.

The Transformation

Here a general shift moves through the assembly, as the sisters off to the side begin to walk from the alcove to the center of the room. The priest stands, the song gains strength among them, and some harmony begins to be heard.

The Growing Song

Although the public ministering of the Congregation has been exhausted, as the women communicate, the song of their lives gathers in power and beauty. The song is a simple one, "God is Love." It swells notably, harmony developing and becoming strong and rich. It is repeated in rounds. At the Offertory, the four "Dream Team" organizers come forward to present to the Leadership of the

Congregation an offering: an artistically designed binder with a complete record of every step of the yearlong project. As the song of their lives opens up, there are some tears and many smiles. Feelings transformed from anxiety to enthusiastic joy. There is a desire to help, inclusive love, and a joyous feeling. Their Chapter dream experience is now complete.

The Bosch family closure was much shorter and simpler. It touched on the deep experience of relationships in the tribe and brought conclusion to the dream project almost a year to the day of its beginning. Held within the usual Sunday brunch setting, it began with a review of feelings and learning associated with the experience. Unlike other tribes accustomed to being in the public eye, their willingness to share a family transformation meant a movement beyond the safety and privacy of family. Also unlike the others, I had prepared this closure ritual from the images, dreams and life experiences which they had shared with me, and had tested it out before hand with John and Marianne.

Remembering their response to the oak tree which their parents had planted in the front yard years before, I chose that image as central to their ritual. Each sibling was sent into the yard both to select an acorn and to plant it in a chosen spot. It was a misty autumn day, but each soon returned and named where s/he had staked a claim. Then John and Marianne drew them into a circle and spoke each daughter's or son's name with this blessing: "Lori, (Joe, Johnny, Tess, David) we ask your forgiveness for any way in which we as your parents may have hurt you. We forgive you for any mistakes you may have made. And now we bless you for your journey into life ahead, in the name of the Father/Mother God, The Son, and the Holy Spirit." The children reciprocated with a spontaneous and loving embrace of their parents. Joe spoke for his siblings when he declared their love for their parents.

Conclusion

"Playing" with symbols becomes a doorway into insight and celebration. Metaphor opens up a new place of feeling. It assists instinctual responses to move from confusion to clarity, from the hidden realm of the unconscious to the conscious world where action can be taken. Here transformation depends on the cooperation of dreamer(s) who must release the tendency to control, and to ignore or resist the dream experience, for its meaning will freely unfold.

Commitment to meaning must at the end be expressed by responsibility for acting in the outer reality. Such action, created ritually, frequently unfolds deeper significance. If the meaning is clear to begin with, the action may be even more direct as the tribe makes a decision to live out its inner transformation. If individuals have left financially comfortable jobs for less remunerative ones, or undertaken an adventurous spiritual enterprise, so also must communities take new steps when this kind of action is a faith response to God's word within them. Freedom and inner peace are its fruits.

CHAPTER NINE

What We Learned Of Dreams, Ourselves, and Our Tribes

I am looking at a program cover with several blocked sections, nicely design-ed. One section is a temple, one a school, one a church, and a —? This is unclear, but feels important.

There are many people moving through a large area or estate. I see a hillside with iris trying to grow through very dry soil. It is Lillian's iris patch. When I poke my finger through the dry soil, there is much moisture underneath. I ask if someone will take care of it.

Then the iris patch becomes a small tank of water with a very large turtle swimming in it. I am afraid the children will be hurt by the turtle. Sister Mary John comes along and is willing to take care of the iris and the turtle.

We are planning for some kind of program or summer school. I am in a library asking for certain books. The one I am looking for is there and a child points it out (Past Dream 033089.1 - <u>The Iris Patch Program</u>, Pat B.).

In retrospect, this dream, coming soon before the first community dream proj-ect, both predicts and summarizes what is about to happen. It touches upon the elements of what a community learns in entering its dreams; moreover, for me as researcher, it traces the stages of my explorations toward completing the work.

Sometimes it is difficult for the dreamer to separate a personal role in the development of the dream research proper from the community dream significance. This was most obvious in the case of the Bosch family where the small number, seven, and the intimate connections of daily life blend each person's transition into the communal soul so that they are almost indistinguishable. It is as if both meanings lie within one another, as they indeed do in the actual unfolding; they are so inextricably tied together. A direct review of Jung's concept of four stages of a dream, will perhaps provide the best summary of what the four tribes of this book have learned in their tribal dream experiences.[53]

Robert Johnson applies the four stages to all dreams, and this dream especially lends itself as model through 1) statement of place, a kind of setting of the psyche, in this case, the context of the community soul; 2) development of the "plot," or the complication at hand; 3) culmination, which hints at how to work on the issue, or at the transformation in progress; and finally, 4) the result, or outcome of the dream work.[54] The opening and closing "program" scenes of the dream above act as bookends for the central revelation of the dream.

The Setting of the Dream

The first scene indicates the dimensions of knowledge which have opened up, neatly blocked out as in the organization of the dream research: the spiritual, academic, relational, and a final undefined block. The dreams frequently yield, in symbolic form, a description of the community "psyche" or situation at the time. In the dream above, the temple represents the *spiritual* knowledge that was gained, the deep new trust in God's word as spoken through the medium of dreams. For the Christian community, the most important value for pursuing the question of community dreams must finally lie in the search for the Kingdom of God. Any other motive makes light of our belief in God's word and life within us. The dreams themselves have taught us about our limitations, and reassured us of God's love in the midst even of our "marks and stains."

Academic knowledge and psychological research, represented by the school, has provided a foundation for understanding and communicating our religious experience. Carl Jung's work invites us to be penetrated by ancient Christian symbols that *already* belong to us. It is not only faith that has assisted in reclaiming our heritage, but myriad scholars, who have prepared the way by their inquiry and experimentation, bolstering the learning which enhance our faith. While this is especially true in the disciplines of psychology, anthropological research into Native American ways and indigenous peoples' lives has also provided another window into dream practice. The greatest learning, however, is that which has been drawn from the very fiber of our human nature, our own experience.

114

Thus the communities have seen that dreams mediate the word of God residing in the core of their reality; in fact, the actuality of community life has been described and affirmed in dreams. Through liberation from rationalization and analysis, members are free to interpret meaning together in the nonrational playful ways of the right brain. It seems appropriate, therefore, to accept the program image of the *church* as relational, since among the many rich symbols of the church the "People of God" has been a major metaphor. The traditional importance of this designation was underlined as the one chosen for a contemporary understanding by the Vatican II documents.[55] Church as relationship has been key as communities pass through the crucial transitions of our times.

For instance, New Jerusalem first traversed a passage characterized by its formation in a clerically-based church, and was then led to another passage in which responsibility rests on lay leadership. I am acutely aware of the Catholic struggle to move from this first style of authority to the second. In the wider church the second style is being experimented with, but the experimentation barely touches the core of the Church's existence! Aligned with that experience, New Jerusalem has moved from a foundational stage of church community—learning responsibility and active participation from a highly charismatic priest—to the full reality of trying to live it. Collegiality and subsidiarity are high ideals, and the future will reveal whether the authority of this community will be willing to continue to take the responsibility for this style of relationship. Will they fall back into some form of dependent relationship of a past style? Will they, like many others, adopt the cynicism and disillusionment of those who have left the formal church, *or* will they rebuild the firm foundation of a church based on the union of ordinary people of faith and good conscience? Dreaming together has created an expansive communal bonding.

Recognition arises, then, that the dream message received by an individual has meaning not only for others, but even goes beyond their respective tribes. In order to function within their destinies, the tribes learn to depend on and to be depended on by other forces of the cosmos. In the dream of this concluding chapter, there is, therefore, a *vague block* on the program cover of the first scene. The "as-yet-unknown" dimension of the communal soul will remain unknown not because of poor dream recall on the dreamer's part; rather, this vagueness indicates that the nature of the unconscious—and of the future—is mysterious, often undefined or unrecognized, never completely plumbed. It will always be so. Frequently during their dream experimenting, communities were to experience the underground connections of the unconscious alternately as threatening, delightful, or inviting. The unconscious holds the ongoing store of both the personal and the collective life. Our human limitations and the demands of the conscious life prevent us from perceiving all of its content and secrets at any one time. Moreover, the limitless depths of revelation of the God within are so intertwined with our human experience that we risk confusion or illusion if we attempt to separate one from the other.

What we did learn, then, is that this container of the unconscious will release its treasures in measured amounts. Although the dreams carried personal meaning for dreamers, we have become convinced that one layer of the ordinary dream will always reveal the community dimension of that person's life. This community element will be all the clearer within persons for whom community is a vitalizing factor of life. Each research tribe has put this community element to work for a deeper knowledge of the community and for its guidance.

The Complication or Issue at Hand

Near the iris patch many people are moving through a large estate. For the Christian intentional community the discovery of dreams as source of God's revelation is truly a new large expanse. Hillsides provide a higher view so that the individual is placed within the wider range of the church and the world. For the dreamer, this may be the expanse of one's life as a community person: first in a family of origin, then as a professional person, and finally as a committed member of a particular religious group.

The difficulty here is that the iris is trying to grow through very dry soil. In the case of the Ursulines of Bruno, the insecurity and helplessness of finding themselves greatly reduced in numbers, and fearing for their future may have deterred them for some time from permitting the waters of new life to be discovered. New Jerusalem, at the beginning of the dream project, was struggling to again trust God's Spirit in its life. It was caught in the dry soil of its own outer reality, its conscious world. For Joseph's sisters, the reality of their position as women in the Church may have been hidden in the unconscious in part because of their loyalty to the Church and their deep habit of obedience and service. And the perfectionist tendency among the Bosch tribe may have, at first, masked their movement from one expression of it to another.

The institutional church, itself a struggling community, is still seeking proper soil for contemporary growth. The dry soil may indicate the difficulty of attaining the wisdom that guided the early Church. This soil prevents the flowering that has, for such a long time and so frequently, blossomed in its garden. But then, not to worry, this is Lillian's patch!

Lillian is a very old neighbor woman with a very green thumb. Both her name and the iris itself refer to the lily, a flower designating purity and resurrection. Most community members discovered that some persons among them had a green thumb for causing dreams to flower and bear fruit. Some more than others seem to be prone to receive "big" dreams. Part of the research dilemma was to convince everyone in a community that they are able to develop new levels of spiritual and psychic powers. Those who actively participated, and trusted their dream life to communal discernment, expressed astonishment at the revelations that their dreams provided for all of us. They came to believe that even an ordinary dream has a community dimension, not limited by our chronological sense of time and space.

The dream suggests an answer to the community dilemma of dryness and lack of awareness. It is the membership that dares to poke into things and find that water is available in the underground of the unconscious. The unconscious is that place of contact with the God-within, so members have experienced being bonded on a deeper level there. Even more, since water is the source of life, a breakthrough is promised in this image. While relearning the worth of being connected with that underground stream, *someone* is needed to care for the iris patch if the garden is to be nourished and brought back to full life.

Ways to Work on a Complication or Issue

As in many dreams within each collection, a wise person appears to render messages from the unconscious or to provide inspiration and guidance (NJ8, NJ98, Other Dream 030390, SSJ83, UBC33). Sister Mary John is a spunky old nun—a literate, pure-hearted New Englander with a care for all that is fragile and in need of assistance. She comes along in response to the membership's asking for help, and is willing to care for both the iris and the turtle; in doing this, she protects the children, our vulnerable selves.

For the poking around is enough to bring the underground water above ground. It has become conscious in the image of the small delineated tank of water. It is now visible and manageable. Members have learned that poking around is a way we must work—or play—with the dreams to make the water available to our conscious reality. Asking for help brings the wisdom guides that are needed. Henry Reed was the first to guide my own explorations, offering the fruits of his own poking around. The dream discerners, themselves, dived fearlessly into the waters of the unconscious, pulling up sunken treasures, polishing them off and offering them as gifts of beauty to their tribes. In return, members offered their dreams, enthusiastically or tentatively. Some went so far as to engage in a Spring Symbol Celebration, in a rite of prayer, or in a display of their dreams captured as art. Some even dramatized the dreams.

Only Wisdom has the knowledge of experience and the guts to care for the turtle! Each community may choose its own closeness to, or distance from, the tank. After all, that turtle is quite large, quite threatening. But through it all, the "voice of the turtle"—traditional Christian symbolism for the voice of the Holy Spirit—"is heard in the land." [56] So we have learned we have nothing to fear. The turtle is swimming in archetypal androgyny: a wonderful union of both feminine and masculine that have been raised to greater awareness. Jung's study of the turtle symbol led him to posit that the turtle represents adult endurance and discerning slowness. These qualities are appropriately applicable to dream work, since a dream may not open itself until many months after the first explorations. The slow turtle carries its shell, its home, like a backpack. It, too, like every spiritual seeker, is on eternal pilgrimage.

117

It is important to note transformation symbols, which often appear in this third section of a dream. One transformation here is the shift of the water from underground, undefined in content and extent, to water above ground, in the defined space of the tank. Such a movement from the unconscious to the conscious reality indicates a process typical of a rite of passage. Every passage participates in liminality, the nature of which is ambiguity and paradox. In this process the environment of the past fades, yet the newly developing milieu is not yet clear in its structure or meaning.

A second shift of symbols occurs as the wise old woman changes from Lillian to Sister Mary John. The first is a very elderly neighbor who draws forth flowers from the earth, the other a nun with a vow of poverty. Victor Turner, who relates the nature of liminality to poverty, says:

> A further . . . characteristic of transitional beings is that they have nothing. They have no status, property, insignia, secular clothing, rank, kinship position, nothing to demarcate them structurally from their fellows. Their condition is indeed the very prototype of sacred poverty.[57]

These two transformation symbols—from Lillian to Sister Mary John, and from the underground water to the small tank of water—describe the entire period in which a community in transition finds itself. It describes a tribe in the throes of need, destructuring, or searching for identity, with only beginning glimpses of hope and re-structuring. However, as Catholic participants in the larger life of Christianity and a changing world, it is scarcely possible to conceive of a near future when the Catholic community will experience any definitive conclusion to its present liminal state.

The Outcome Leads to the Future

"We" are planning summer school. At the time of the dream, I was seeking June approval of my research plan; but, as a *community* image, the dream image opening Chapter One reoccurs: "Summer" is a happy place of simple community respite and support. A whole library is available, whether it is spiritual, academic, or relational—or even vague or undefined—in content. But it takes the openness and honesty of the child in the community soul to point out the exact "book." The conclusion of a dream frequently points to the future.

So this book, like the dream, concludes where all life begins: in the potential of a Child. In New Jerusalem's drama of a treasure hunt dream, it is the *children* who hold the clues to discovering the priesthood of the people. It is the essence of a community's beginnings that "new children" strip the clothes off the institutional church and reveal her unadorned beauty (NJ 44, SSJ59, UBC5).

The wise woman is simply another face of the Divine Child who leads us, in wisdom and endurance, to recognize and claim the transforming existence at the very center of who we are. To paraphrase the ending to the Gospel of John: It is the community of God's people who testifies to these things and has written them, and we know that this testimony is true.[58] There are many dreams that the Spirit of Jesus has given, but if these were to be listed one by one, I do not think the whole world could contain the words God has given in our unconscious.

> *Then I notice that the children are in the center of the circle in a mythical, magical jungle gym, and they begin to sing like angels!!! You can't see them, but they are singing in ethereal harmony; they are also playing various bells. It's WONDERFUL!!!*
>
> *This helps me decide that I would like to live here* (Dream 83.032590 - <u>Life in the Commune</u>, Barb G.).

Section C

RESOURCES AND GUIDELINES

NOTES

Introduction

[1] Carl G. Jung, *The Collected Works of Carl G. Jung*, "Psychoanalysis and the Cure of Souls," ed. Sir Herbert Read, et al., Bollingen Series, 20 vol. (New York: Princeton University Press, 1970), vol.11, 353. All subsequent references to the works of Carl G. Jung will be taken from this edition. The abbreviation CW will be used.

[2] An intentional community is one formed by the deliberate choice of its members to be together around common values and common goals, giving rise to a lifestyle of specific commitment mechanisms. Patricia Wittberg in her reflection on traditional religious life, *Creating a Future of Religious Life: A Sociological Perspective* (Mahwah, N.J.: Paulist Press, 1991), p.4, defines an intentional community as one in which members cede control over some or all aspects of both their public and private lives.

[3] Louis Savary et al, *Dreams and Spiritual Growth: A Judeo-Christian Way of Dreamwork* (New York: Paulist Press, 1984). Savary and his colleagues develop a thorough outline of the use and effectiveness of dreams in scripture, as well as in the following centuries of Christianity. Dreams were honored and attended to until the late Middle Ages, when the Age of Reason began.

[4] C. G. Jung, CW, v.12, *Psychology and Alchemy*, "Individual Dream Symbolism in Relation to Alchemy,"
p. 71.

[5] Ibid., v.10, 296-300.

[6] C. G. Jung, CW, v.10, *Civilization in Transition*, "The Undiscovered Self (Present and Future)," 296ff.

[7] Jeremy Taylor, *Dream Work: Techniques for Discovering the Creative Power in Dreams* (New York: Paulist Press, 1993) p. 11ff.

[8] David Shipler, *Arab and Jew: Wounded Spirits in a Promised Land* (New York: New York Times Books, 1992).

[9] Henry Reed, Ph.D., *Sundance: The Community Sundance Journal*, "The Sundance Experiment." Nos. 1-4, 1976-1979. Out of Print, but available on the internet at www.creativespirit.net/sundancedreamjournal.

[10] Cada, Lawrence, et al, *Shaping the Coming Age of Religious Life* (New York: Seabury Press, 1979).

[11] Watkins, Susan, *Dreaming Myself, Dreaming A Town* (New York: Kendall Enterprises, 1989).

Chapter One

[12] Many Christians understand Community as God's gift. Dietrich Bonhoeffer, in *Life Together* (New York: Harper and Row, 1954, p. 19ff), points out the effect of physical presence on Christians in community. But community is more than a way to be together, more than a support system. Evelyn and James Whitehead have studied Christian faith communities in light of the contemporary American search for an authentic socially conscious shared life. In *Community of Faith: Models and Strategies for Developing Christian Communities* they state, "Community is a goal of social life; it points to the possibility of a shared vision that can move us into action in a public sphere, undertaken in a context of mutual concern" (Minneapolis, MN: Seabury Press, 1982). They continue with a warning, "There is sometimes a tendency, perhaps even a temptation, among religious people to think of community exclusively in its primary group connotation. But surely the Christian witness of working together unceasingly to hasten the coming of the Kingdom stands equal to the Christian witness we bear one another as a sign to the world of God's presence among us" (Ibid., p. 32).

[13] Bernard Lee and Michael Cowan, *Dangerous Memories: House Churches and Our American Experience* (Kansas City: Sheed and Ward, 1986).

[14] The image of the sick adolescent appeared in a dream of 1990. Like most dreams of any importance this one has several layers of meaning which may apply differently at different times. The sick adolescent speaks to the many hurting young people who came to the community; it also speaks to the condition of the larger church. In 1990 it was part of a series of dreams which depicted community stages of growth through pregnancy, birth, childhood, and in this case, adolescence.

[15] Luke 24 : 32

[16] The title of a paperback book about the very early days of New Jerusalem, written by Sister Gus Taurish, published by Whitaker House in 1975. Gus was then a Glenmary sister, briefly associated with the community's beginnings. She was a hearty and high-spirited woman in love with Francis's call to the poor.

[17] The once dying neighborhood, however, in these past twenty years has been renewed, refurbished and integrated. Now it is a mix of the old German working class families who first settled the area, African-Americans and Appalachians. Some persons who grew up there have returned, and local churches have united

for shared prayer, meals, and neighborhood service. As New Jerusalem members arrived in relatively large numbers, they often obtained the most rundown houses and restored them, resulting in less transience and more stability. We were once "accused" of raising property values, and we recognize the dangers of transferring our upper middle class values to a place chosen for its simplicity.

[18] "Whoever does not accept the kingdom of God like a child will not enter it" (Luke 18:17).

[19] Richard emphasized the meaning of radical as "rooted." This term continues to be helpful in theological reflection as the old categories of conservative and liberal fail to express any perduring sense of gospel perspectives.

[20] Patricia Wittberg, *Creating a Future for Religious Life: A Sociological Perspective* (Mahwah, N.J.: Paulist Press, 1991).

[21] One woman described Richard by saying, "He's a little boy with a big gift." For years Richard's resonant voice, immortalized on the hundreds of thousands of tapes of his talks, belied his youthful appearance. When he first began preaching, he arrived at an appointed place where he was thought to be the paper boy coming to collect money.

[22] Henry Reed, Ph. D., launched his dream research at Princeton University and in the sleep laboratory at the C. G. Jung Institute in Zurich. His creative and brilliant work is unfortunately less known than that of other current dream researchers. He teaches and continues to conduct psychical research at the Association for Research and Enlightenment (A.R.E.) in Virginia Beach, Virginia. His books, tapes and videos can be obtained directly from him on his website at www.creativespirit.net/henryreed or by writing to him at 3777 Fox Creek Road, Mouth of Wilson, VA 24363; (800) 398-1370. He is the only person whom I have identified as doing extensive research on community dreaming.

[23] Taped private interview with Henry Reed, December, 1988.

[24] In *Habits of the Heart* (New York: Harper&Row, 1986), Robert Bellah and his colleagues discuss the problems of American individualism and self-interest which threaten to undermine the civic good.

[25] The leadership process provided for a first level of nomination by all members of the community from among those who have lived in community for six years or more. Five votes are needed to remain in nomination. On a second nomination from among these persons, ten to twelve persons with the largest number of votes go away for a weekend with a facilitator. In prayer and a discernment process, they select the final leadership from among their group.

Chapter Two

[26] Book of Genesis, Chapters 37-50.

[27] Gertrude Jobes, *Dictionary of Mythology, Folklore, and Symbols* (New York: Scarecrow Press, 1962) v. I, 603, 296-7, 6060, 456-8; v. II, 1688.

[28] The Dream Reference Guide at the end of the book gives a larger context of each dream referred to below. If the reader would like to pursue these, this process is used throughout the text.

Chapter Three

[29] <u>CW</u>, v.7, *Two Essays on Analytic Psychology*, "The Relations Between the Ego and the Unconscious,"
147-8.

[30] Henry Reed, Ph.D., *Sundance: The Community Sundance Journal*, v. 1, "The Sundance Experiment: An Introduction," 1976. Out of Print, but available on the internet at www.creativespirit.net/sundancedreamjournal.

Chapter Four

[31] The Path of Adult Transformation

WHO ARE WE NOW? IMAGES		
John	stairway	going up, light through open door at top
	paw print	bear, strong and nurturing
Lori	clown	entertaining, but often sad; people scared of clowns because they don't know what's underneath (Shadow)
Joe	couch	comfortable, big, fluffy, homey
Johnny	cherry chest	has a history, rough time but beautiful song
Tess	lion	smart, strong, stick together help one another
	car	always moving someplace, never alone on the road
David	eagle	brought back from being nearly extinct; reminds us we are part of a larger family

Chapter Five

[32] Dr. Thomas Dyehouse, *Silent Messages*, v. ii, 2, Nov., 1997.

[33] In NJ Dream 51.112889 *Out of Refuse, Something Usable*, Tim B. finds some usable insulation in a pile of refuse, an image similar to the basement scene where some good things are taken "up" where they can be used.

[34] CW, v.5, *Symbols of Transformation*, "Introduction,"p. 123.

[35] CW, v.18, "The Symbolic Life," 244-252.

[36] CW, v.14, "Mysterium Coniunctionis," 533-543.

[37] Jeremy Taylor, *Dream Work: Techniques for Discovering the Creative Power in Dreams* (New York: Paulist Press, 1983) 116-142. Taylor lists twenty-five elements common to dreams.

[38] "What is true of humanity in general is also true of each individual, . . . And, as is the psychology of humanity so also is the psychology of the individual." C. G. Jung, CW, v.7, "On the Psychology of the Unconscious," 50. This theme is referred to repeatedly in Jung's works.

[39] CW, v.10, "The Undiscovered Self," 262.

[40] Mircea Eliade, *Images and Symbols: Studies in Religious Symbolism* (San Diego: Harcourt Brace, 1987) p. 345.

[41] Gertrude Jobes, *Dictionary of Mythology, Folklore and Symbols*, v.2. (New York: Scarecrow, 1962).

[42] Paul Shepard, *The Sacred Paw: The Bear in Nature, Myth and Literature* (New York: Viking, 1985).

Chapter Six

[43] See *Bibliographies*, 223.

[44] See *Process Guidelines*, 227.

Chapter Seven

[45] Reed, Henry, Ph.D., *The Community Dream Journal*, "The Sundance Experiment: An Introduction," v.1, no.1, 1976, 108-140.

[46] Henry Reed, a practical theorist, has a unique gift for offering dream techniques that are simple and unthreatening for the ordinary dreamer. For a description of his playful techniques and of the incubation rituals that prepare for dreams, see *Getting Help From Your Dreams* (Virginia Beach, VA: Hermes Home Press, 1995). See note 51.

[47] Jeremy Taylor, *Dream Work: Techniques for Discovering the Creative Power in Dreams* (New York: Paulist Press, 1983) 17ff.

[48] 2 Corinthians 12:9

[49] C. G. Jung, CW, v.9ii, *Aion: Researches into the Phenomenology of the Self*, "The Structure and Dynamics of the Self," 167. The stone appears in many of Jung's works related to the alchemical and religious symbolism of individuation.

[50] The rectangle is a kind of square, and as such, has many complex meanings related to the circle and the meaning of completion. Specific to the New Jerusalem Community is its appearance as the City, a particularly important symbol. See C. G. Jung, CW, v.11, "Psychology and Religion: West and East," "The History and Psychology of a Natural Symbol," 64-5.

Chapter Eight

[51] Reed, Henry, Ph.D., *Getting Help From Your Dreams* (New York: Ballantine Books, 1985). Out of print, but available on the internet at www.creativespirit.net/sundancedreamjournal.Introductory blurb. This book is filled with creative suggestions for honoring and probing dreams.

[52] Adapted from *The Inclusive New Testament*, W. Hyattsville, MD: Priests for Equality, 1994.

Chapter Nine

[53] Mary Ann Matoon, in her book *Understanding Dreams*, does her own development of this concept (Dallas: Spring Publications, 1978).

[54] CW. v8, *The Structure and Dynamics of the Psyche*, "On the Nature of Dreams," para 561-564.

[55] Walter Abbot, S.J., ed. *The Documents of Vatican II*, "Dogmatic Constitution on the Church," New York: Herder&Herder, 1966, 24ff.

[56] Song of Songs 2:12. Many editions of the Bible have translated this variously as "the voice of the turtle," "the voice of the turtle-dove," and the voice of the dove." By the time the twentieth century linguists had arrived at the latter term, the image of the turtle was deep in the Christian psyche.

[57] Victor Turner, in his well-known essay, "Betwixt and Between: The Liminal Period in the Rites of Passage," develops and extends Arnold van Gennup's concept of transition. The quotation appears in the opening chapter of *The Forest of Symbols: Aspects of Ndembu Ritual*, Ithaca, (NY: Cornell University Press, 1970), 8.

58 John 21:24-25

Key: NJ   New Jerusalem, Cincinnati, Ohio
      SSJ   Joseph's Sisters Dream, Nazareth, Michigan
      UBC   Ursulines of Brown County, St. Martin, Ohio
      WOL   Ursuline Way of Life Committee [Belleville,
             Illinois; Louisville, Kentucky; Cincinnati, Ohio,
             and St. Martin, Ohio]
      BRU   Ursulines Of Bruno, Saskatchewan
      BOS   Bosch Family, Edgewood, Kentucky

(NJ) New Jerusalem Dreams, Cincinnati, Ohio

NJ Past Dream 000082 - I am walking east of the Gethsemane monastery, following a creek and asking everyone I pass to show the "most beautiful part of the monastery." It gets darker and darker the farther I go into the woods. I look back and many people are coming after me with rock projectiles coming at me. I turn toward them pleading and not understanding, repeating the same words. One of the rocks hits me and knocks me out.

When I come to, I am alone in the dark woods and very sad. I look into the murky creek, and there are two drowned bodies: a little boy and a little girl. I lift them out of the water and know - either then or when I waken - that they are my feminine side and my spontaneous, free eternal boy. I have let both die in my unconsciousness and running. The grief I feel is immense and lasts for a long time. I waken literally weeping with my heart pumping (NJ Past Dream 000082, The Most Beautiful Part of the Monastery, Richard R.).

NJ 2 - A group of men are on retreat. There are two women about to give birth. A guru comes and blesses the birth (NJ 2.083189B - Birth, Pat B.).

NJ 5 - In my house the inner dream group sleeps. I wake up—people are sleeping in sleeping bags on the floor. I am aware that I have numerous dreams, some of which have no relevance to this dream process. I want to take time before others awaken (NJ 5.083189.E, Searching For Dream Space, Holly F.).

NJ 44 -We are walking outdoors, and it is sort of a treasure hunt; we don't know where we're going. We don't know the way, but we find out one step at a time. THAT IS THE GAME, AND IT IS A LOT OF FUN. . . .WE ARE HAVING A WHEE OF A TIME!

It then seems we are going to [a] Mall, and when we are there we try on costumes, we then realize that they are costumes for Mass, different vestments. They are bright and festive and party-like. We all seem to know that THE VESTMENTS ARE THE TREASURE. We are having a real celebration trying them on ourselves

and each other. (Dream 44.112889.B - <u>The Vestments Are the Treasure,</u> Barb G.).
NJ Other Dream - We are in a prison, a very unhappy place. It is . . . a vast prisoner-of-war camp . . . and we are just a small number of people. . . . We recognize one another but are not permitted to speak or to embrace. All we do is our work, and follow the regimen. . . . As a way of keeping prisoners satisfied and quiet, the guards reward those who cooperate with fancy clothes, treasure of gold and silver. And those who refuse to cooperate, those who are unable to work so hard, are deprived of these treasures. . . . No on has time for quiet or conversation or reflection, because piped into the prison is a steady stream of commercials.

And through it all this longing persists within us for some contact with each other. Then someone has an idea and passes the word around in quiet whispers so that others can't hear "Seven-thirty! Seven-thirty!" (NB. The time for all NJ community meetings.) Soon people begin to catch on . . . each of us crawls into our cubicle, there we go into prayer and ask "Are you the One, or are we to look for another?"

And the next day as we pass one another in the prison yard we can't speak but we know we have asked the question. And we nod and feel freedom. . . . Our fellow prisoners, . . . find this quite strange, especially as the joy among us begins to grow. . . . Soon even those who had been torturers begin to ask, "Are you the One? Or are we to look for another?" [They care less and less for the clothes and treasures] until, in the end, there is great partying and feasting. The air is filled with jewels and clothes and gold as everyone throws them into the air and tosses them back and forth. The commercials turn to song and dance. And the prison turns into a ballroom (NJ Other, 120289 - "<u>Are You the One Who Is To Come</u>?" Bob G.).

NJ74 - I am at the Istanbul airport in the parking lot near the terminal. There are three pilots in giant electric hand mixers (without beaters) flying around near the tall lights that illuminate the parking lot at night. I explain to Zachary that they can change lightbulbs and make repairs that way (NJ 74.022590 - <u>Electric Energy</u>, Robin M.).

NJ Other - I am walking down a very busy street. Out of one of the doorways Sister Jose Hobday walks up and blocks our path, . . . I am awe-struck . . . I love her. I feel shy, very shy. . . . Jose takes my hand, looks right into my eyes, and says, "Oh, you are a very holy woman." I feel ashamed. I don't feel it is true. I feel very vulnerable, I lower my head. . . . I start to cry and the more I cry, the more I can look into her eyes.

NJ Other Dream 030390 - <u>The Wise Woman Changes the Scene</u>, Patsy W.).
NJ98 - A group of 12 women, wearing long skirts or robes, are standing in a tightly formed circle. Their arms are raised and tilted toward the center of the circle. They pass a baby from one to another (NJ 98, 072290 - <u>The Women's Circle</u>, Ron F.).

(SSJ) Joseph's Sisters, Nazareth, Michigan

SSJ11 - She is being very definite about things that are missing and should have been on [the forms]. I lay there listening and finally say to myself, "Speak up, and say something because it is not all that wrong." I do (SSJ 11, 031993 - Speak Up, Lucy S.).

SSJ21 - Dreamer's Comment on walking about and observing, but not engaged (SSJ 21, 031993 - Mass in the Huge Cathedral, Janice W.).

SSJ29 - a) There is a white light switch and I am going to turn it on. I keep going up to it, but I don't turn it on (SSJ 29, 031993 - Light/ Darkness, Joan M.).

SSJ29 b) When we leave we walk and walk. There is mud and we have to walk through it. We are all upset about getting our clothes and feet dirty. We continue walking and come to a green, grassy area. As we walk we find ourselves in some-one's backyard, a fenced-in yard. There is a gate and it opens for us. Several have already passed through. A few of us are approaching the gate. . . . All of us walk through the gate. It [was] originally locked. We don't know who unlocked it, but we walk through and are safe. The interesting thing is that there is no mud on us and our clothes are clean (SSJ 29, 031993 - Journey, Joan M.).

SSJ35 - We are packing . . . time to move on . . . not sure where. We stop packing and sit on a couch, watching the new, young, vivacious people arrive. They are going to begin their vacation. The hosts are paying attention to the new arrivals, but try to be gracious to us (SSJ 35, 031993 - New Life, Sylvia D.).

SSJ39 Dreamer's Comment on SSJ 39, 031993 - Life and Death Through Animals, Patricia W: Rather than just watching and waiting for life, she (we) enters into it, [into relationship], feelings of acceptance, anticipation, belonging.

SSJ40 -[There] is a table covered with a cloth. Loretta uncovers it and there is a lot of jewelry spread out and we . . . are looking at it thinking we might like to have something and Loretta says, "No, this is for the Church" and she puts it in contain-ers and puts them in a medicine closet like you have in the bathroom (SSJ 50 - Jewels for the Church, Marie B.).

SSJ50 - The sun is shining and it is early morning. I am a participant in this experi-ence, though sleepy—seemingly awakened by the group entering my room. My hair is disheveled. It is hard to get my eyes open (SSJ 50, 031993 - Butterflies and Sunshine, Irene W.).

SSJ52 - We, a large crowd of mostly SSJs, are in a very large church for a meeting. . . . I am in a back row on a chair that is a plastic folding type which feels the "give," but a couple of chairs down is a solid wood chair and I move to it. (SSJ 52, 031993 - Together We Move to "the More", Cheryl A.).

SSJ53 - See Chapter Eight, pp 109-110.

SSJ54 - I am in the same church. . . . I am sitting about five pews back from the front on the right (facing the altar) side (SSJ 54, 031993 - Identical Twins, Emily S).

SSJ57 - In one room the students are being timed for a [math] test. . . . One of the students in that classroom is a sister from our business office. She wants a few more seconds to solve the problem she is working on when time is called. I have a sense of knowing this from the intercom and also being able to see through the glass walls (SSJ 57, 031993 - Reunion, Beth S.).

SSJ58 - I am a train engineer. I and the passengers are getting on at the same door and at the same time. I am trying to find my place to steer the train. The train is going. How am I going to stop it? I am spending time to see where I can see, to observe whether something is ahead (SSJ 58, 031993 - Steering Blindfolded, Edna S.).

SSJ59 - I turn to see a pretty little girl about six or seven years of age moving past me. A few paces ahead, she turns to look back at me, and I note the very sweet but serious expression on her face in that fleeting glance. . . . It puzzles me that she is alone, and yet seems to know where she is going, rather determinedly. . . . I do not follow her but only seem to see her moving down the long bright corridor, . . . a colorful scene which evoked feelings of love, care, and goodness, also trust (SSJ 59, 031993 - A Wandering or Lost Child, Edna S.).

SSJ61 - I begin to help, but I must leave before we are finished as people are waiting for me in the car. When I return to the car there are two unfamiliar women in the back seat who need a ride. I ask them for directions to where they live, but they don't know how to direct me. They don't know what to tell me. I ask them for approximate directions, give me an idea of general area to go to. We begin driving in a general direction (SSJ 61, 031993 - Going Somewhere, Betsy M.).

SSJ62 - I . . . have decided to go into the Catholic Church just ahead of me. The door pushes to my right off the sidewalk. I'm feeling delighted and awed at entering into a brightly lighted, airy, high-ceilinged large room. There is a bustling movement and quiet excitement ahead of me as I glance over the space to find a place. There are no pews, but blue-cushioned chairs with kneelers. I'm walking toward a chair but several persons are waving me away. . . . I choose a seat in the back and am looking toward the front where the action is. The chairs in back are facing the aisle rather than the altar. Though we're in the back, I get the feeling that we are contented where we are (SSJ 62, 031993 - <u>A Day in Chicago</u>, Katie K.).

SSJ63 - I see reconciliation to each other. There are people from work and sisters. Sr. M. waits for me. I am late for an appointment. She is patient, gentle and affirming. There is something about two [younger sisters]. The computer is "messed up" by the youth minister. Now nobody shares or helps or cares. I put on my new black coat, . . . and go home. I won't be a savior if nobody cares (SSJ 63, 031993 - <u>Not A Savior</u>, Janet C.).

SSJ70 - I'm in some kind of night club with my niece, Janine. I want to ask her to look at my incision to see if it's healing normally. I'm now in [a] bedroom in the nightclub. Janine comes in bed with me. My brother, Everett, opens the door and says to us, "Hurry up. It's 10:30 already. We have to meet the others for brunch." I can't find my clothes. Everett is grabbing things to hurry me along. I'm in my robe. Janine still hasn't looked at my cut from my biopsy. I'm telling Everett, "I still have to dream. Wait . . ." (SSJ 70, 031993 - <u>Looking for the White Car</u>, Joyce D.).

SSJ77 - I am living at my parents' house. . . . All of a sudden, a customer from the bank I used to work at pops his head in through the window. "Norm!" I exclaim. "How are you? What are you doing here?" "I am here ready for the demonstration." I stick my head out the window. On the roof, I see about a dozen folding chairs set up for the men to occupy. My father is out there on the roof with some other middle aged men whom I don't know. They're discussing plans for the demonstration. "This isn't going to get violent, is it?" I ask. "Well, we hope not, but you never know. We're preparing just in case," my Dad answers. "Why does it have to get violent? There is no purpose to having both sides end up getting hurt. It's a useless waste of lives. Dad, come on in. I don't want you to get hurt. Cancel this demonstration" I plead (SSJ 77, 031993 - <u>The Demonstration</u>, Karen G.).

SSJ78 - I am preparing to go somewhere with some of my SSJ friends. We seem to be taking our time, it is early morning (SSJ 78, 031993 - <u>Remember Where You Came From</u>, Mary Ann McC.).

SSJ83 - Then I see on a piece of paper the signature of [a] sister who I had not yet met. . . . I began to talk to the Dominicans and they begin to talk about one of their sisters who . . . is a tower of a woman, both in size and heart. She has an extraordinary ability to gather the sisters around her wherever she goes and form them into a wonderful, loving community where they really love one another and support one another, are filled with the gospel fervor, with the Word of the Lord, and so importantly direct all their energies as one loving, tremendous force into the ministry and are remarkably fruitful. . . . We are talking about what enables her to do this and other Dominicans are telling me about a motto, a core saying in their community, which this sister lives out so perfectly. I can see an emblem which each of them wears over their hearts. It is like a heart but full of Light, an intense white Light burning in the center of each of these emblems and the "saying," the "motto," has to do with going through the center of this heart, this intense, living Light, passing through to the other side. Then I see the sister we are talking about, a large towering woman but with a very gentle face and she says very simply, "I passed through." I understand that she has entered into the eye and heart of the community symbol (SSJ83, 031993 - <u>Your Dream</u>, Marcella C.).

Ursuline Sisters Dreams

(UBC) Ursulines of Brown County, St. Martin, Ohio

UBC5 - I have no idea what is going to happen. Then from a left central door comes a line of children, from ages ten to twelve. . . . They are smiling delightedly, hurrying tiptoe as though to take the audience by surprise. Their bodies are bent forward slightly, for they are trying to keep out of sight, and they are wriggling with anticipation. . . . as I stand perplexed, I glimpse Martha W. away up front, leading the line. Her forefinger is close to her mouth in a shushing gesture. Her face is serious, but still it is relaxed into a half smile, as though in sympathy with the children's project and their glee (UBC 5, 061992 - <u>Passageways to the Song</u>, Miriam T.).

UBC9 - I am dressed in green and wearing white shoes. I am on my way to our annual Social Justice meeting in Washington, DC. I am on foot, having consciously chosen to leave the car behind. I come upon a hill in the woods through which I am walking. The hill is covered with snow. I pull myself over the steep hill by going sideways and grasping bushes, tree limbs, whatever I can grab hand-over-hand as I ascend the hill. I reach the top not out of breath with my clothes and shoes untouched. By the way, under the snow all the bushes and leaves on the trees are in full bloom (UBC 9, 061992 - <u>Moving Into God's Eye</u>, Chrissie P.).

UBC26 - I am in a new car. I can't describe it except that it is new. I am leaving Good Samaritan [Hospital]. I am driving but the accelerator is wobbly. I can't seem to get it steady. My foot keeps trying. But it is so frustrating. I am so concerned that the car is going to scrape against the walls on either side as I try to exit. Sr. Angela is in the car. She is very supportive. . . . As I finally get the pedal and go forward I reach the end of the drive, but there is a pile of shining bright white stones blocking any attempt to go forward. So I must back up. I am concerned again for the car, and that it will be so hard to go into reverse with this pedal. And also the narrow curving driveway between the stone walls. However, Angela keeps encouraging me and I put my foot on the pedal and begin to progress backward (UBC 26, 061992 - <u>Leaving the Hospital</u>, Mary D.).

UBC31 - As I sit in the community I feel the community as a pregnant woman who is ready to give birth. The pains of labor have started and she is not responding to them. She concentrates on the discussion that is going on around her and hopes that if she can ignore the pains that they will go away. The pains continue and grow in severity. To one looking on, it is difficult to know that this woman is in labor; she is so controlled (UBC 31, 061992 - The Pregnant Virgin, Carolyn S.).

UBC33 - It is summer and the setting is colorful. We are outside, . . . when Judy M. hears "Them" coming. . . . Then we see what she sees: huge giants in the distance, . . . a group of women coming over the hills, stepping carefully even in their transparent state. They are dressed in gray with gray bonnets. As they come closer, they become smaller in size. . . . When they reach and embrace Judy near the river, they are life-size and solid, having bodies like ours. . . . I experience a wave of awareness which I feel deeply [when saying good-bye]: this is a visitation of the foundresses; they had come to visit, share joy, encourage and comfort (UBC 33, 061792 - A Visitation By the Foundresses, Lucy S.).

(WOL) Ursuline Way of Life Committee

[Belleville, Illinois; Louisville, Kentucky;
Cincinnati, Ohio, and St. Martin, Ohio]

WOL2 - I see my own face. The left side . . . is peeling away in layers. It is scary (WOL 1, 112894 - My Own Face, Mary Ellen).

WOL3 - I am sharing a huge room with a family. I desire to be incorporated with them. The family is in a king-sized bed together. The mother is very ill, gets out of bed with great effort to make me a sandwich (WOL 3, 112894 - In Bed Together, Anne Maureen M.).

WOL4 - I am standing where Vine Street forks into Jefferson Avenue on the left. I will take the Jefferson turn, where traffic runs smoothly leading into the lovely residential area on Ludlow. It will be easier that way. Straight in front is the heavily trafficked Vine Street, with several traffic lights within a short distance. It is less convenient, passes Veterans Hospital on the right and the Zoo at the next curve. It then proceeds down through a poor residential area. Extensive hospital facilities on the right of this whole area, and the University complex on the left (WOL 2, 112894 - The Fork in the Road, Pat B.).

(BRU) Ursulines Of Bruno, Saskatchewan, Canada

BRU23 - I am in a place without life. It is a dry land in which the earth is caked, hard, and without humus. . . . So the flowers dry up and the trees don't produce fruits, and the spring which has been so lovely has lost its beauty. . . . I say to myself: "If this garden were mine I would make a variety of changes: fertilize the land, replant the flowers and care for the spring with tenderness."

Time passes . . . I notice changes in the garden: thriving plants and a spring that forms a beautiful waterfall and when the sun shines on it, it produces a lovely rainbow. Each time as I know the garden better, I feel that I am being transformed with it . . . the tree is giving its first fruits. I see a woman with a smile so welcoming. She says: "Come, be part of this garden. You can care for it well." As I love very much flowers, roses, etc., my joy is immense. I become responsible for a part of the garden (BRU 23, 112596) - The Garden Re-blooms, Ana D.).

(BOS) Bosch Family, Edgewood, Kentucky

BOS3 - I am playing shortstop during a baseball game. I hear dad yell, "Quit playing in the dirt, son" (BOS 3, 102697 - Shortstop David B.).

BOS4 - Smashing pumpkins. Song - Beautiful, you're beautiful as the sun. Wonderful, you're wonderful as they come. Prodigy song - violence hitting people. Tears are joyful, sad, mad. All by myself. Nobody is there (BOS 4, 102697 - Two Songs, Johnny B.).

BOS7 - I am approaching a big, lovely, old home, probably 100-150 years old. I see a small path that, although it is a bit out of the way, will lead me to this same room.

I begin to walk, feeling very peaceful and enjoying the beauty of nature, when suddenly, I hear a deep growl. Uh-oh, a dog - and not a friendly one. I remember that if I behave calmly and back off without making any sudden moves, I'll be safe. Slowly I lay down my purse and begin to move back the way I came. The dog (a yellow one!) walks parallel with me growling the whole time.

I make it safely to the dream group and tell everyone my story. As we begin to settle down, . . . I begin to feel nervous, hesitant, apprehensive as I realize that I am going to have to SPEAK UP and tell (the facilitator) I am going to get my purse. I am also quite fearful of going out there by that damn dog again! I do speak up and I do go get my purse but I don't go alone. I take someone with me from the group. A man, I think . . . . I rescue my purse. I also take my own dog which overpowers the yellow dog. I feel very secure in my mission with these two by my side (BOS 7, 102797 - The Barking Dog, Marianne B.).

BOS8 - I'm walking through my school and then by the soccer field where my team plays. I can move my nose from side to side. I can make the tip of it touch my left side and then my right side. That doesn't hurt, it only hurts when it lines up perfectly down the middle of my face (BOS 8, 102897 - Who Nose? Johnny B.).

BOS11 - I am one of a large group. There is a feeling of danger. Not like the building might blow up, but that someone is trying to keep us there against our will. I have a plan. Since that someone is not with us at the moment, I think we can escape. I propose this idea to the group . . . as I leave, others start to follow. I get outside the building to what looks like a back parking lot. Those who have joined me are all women. (Of course, the men aren't going to follow some stupid blond woman.)

We decide to walk away fast. Then, suddenly, we are in my mom's van. I am thinking to myself . . . someone will find out that we are in it. And, for whatever reason, we do not want to be discovered (BOS 11, 102297 - On the Run, Lori B.).

BOS13 - I run down the stairs as fast as I can. I go to my kitchen, grab two cups and a pop tart. One cup is orange juice and one is milk. I have the two cups in one hand and the pop tart in the other hand. I run to our garage and outside to the car. I say, "Come on, we have to leave" (BOS 13,103197 - Two Cups, Johnny B.).

BOS14 - I am ready to go out with some friends. I put my seatbelt on and just pray that we get to our destination safely. We pick up five people. I am getting out though, no matter how many people are in the car (BOS 14b, 110397 - Cruisin', Lori B.).

BOS16 - I am asked to model a costume at the high school that I attended. My son, Joseph, is there at the time and he comments how I am embarrassing him. I do not remember modeling (BOS 16, 110697, John Models, John B.).

BOS20 - As I am walking alone to a business meeting, I am talking with people I meet along the way. . . . At the meeting, I am called upon by the moderator to be the person who holds the microphone which is a Cross pen. I walk from table to table as the different attendees state who they are and where they are from (BOS 20, 110997 - The Business Man, John B.).

BOS26 - I find an old jewelry box of mine, there is a lot of jewelry in it. What catches my eye is a ring that has a brownish colored round stone. There is also a necklace or a bracelet that matches it. They might have been my grandmother's jewelry. I am delighted to find this . . . jewelry. I put the ring on; it is beautiful and will go well with any outfit. This ring could make a boring outfit exciting (BOS 26, 111797 - Long Lost..., Lori B.).

BOS27 - I am in Biggs store. The building is much larger than normal. I am looking for Chris . . . everything looks different (BOS 27, 111897 - Same Old Store, Different Look, Lori B.).

BOS28 - I am with my boyfriend, Tom, in his bedroom. I look at his bed and notice that it's very sloppy. This is unusual. Tom is very particular about how his bed is made. I am shocked to say the least. I ask him why his bed looks like this and his response is very indifferent. I decide to fix it myself (BOS 28, 111897 - <u>The Slacker</u>, Lori B.).

A. General Bibliography of Dreams and Images

Bolen, Jean Shinoda, M.D. *Goddesses in Every Women*. Cambridge: Harper Colophon, 1984.

Bosnak, Robert. *Tracks in the Wilderness of Dreaming*. New York: Delacorte Press, 1996.

Claremont de Castillejo, Irene. *Knowing Woman: A Feminine Psychology*. New York: Harper Colophon Books, 1973.

Clift, Jean Dalby and Wallace B. *Symbols of Transformation in Dreams*. New York: Crossroad, 1987.

Dolnick, Edward. *The Atlantic Monthly*. "What Dreams Are (Really) Made Of." (July, 1990): 41-61.

Eckhart, Meister. *Parabola, Journal of Myth and Tradition*. "Where Is He That is Born?" XX1, 2 1996.

Eliade, Mircea. *The Sacred and the Profane: The Nature of Religion*. San Diego: Harcourt Brace, 1987.

Estes, Clarissa Pinkola, Ph.D. *Women Who Run With the Wolves*. New York: Ballantine, 1992.

Fincher, Susanne F. *Creating Mandalas for Insight, Healing and Self-Expression*. Boston: Shambala, 1991.

Fromm, Erich. *The Forgotten Language, An Introduction to Dreams, Fairy Tales and Myths*. New York: Grove Press, 1951.

Garfield, Patricia. *Creative Dreaming*. Ballantine Books, 1974.

Gutheil, Emil A.,M.D. *The Handbook of Dream Analysis*. New York: Liveright, 1951.

Guzie, Tad and Noreen Monroe. *About Men and Women*. New York: Paulist Press, 1986.

Hall, James A., M.D. *Jungian Dream Interpretation*. Toronto: Inner City Books, 1983.

Hillman, James. *Common Boundary: Between Spirituality and Psychotherapy*. "Soul and Spirit," Nov-Dec, 1992.

Hurley, Katherine and Dobson, Theodore. *My Best Self: Using the Enneagram to Free the Soul*. San Francisco: Harper, 1993.

Johnson, Robert A. *He: Understanding Masculine Psychology*. New York: Harper and Row, 1989.
_____. *She: Understanding Feminine Psychology*. Perennial Library, 1989.

_____. *We: Understanding the Psychology of Romantic Love*. San Francisco: Harper and Row, 1983.

_____. *Inner Work*. San Francisco: Harper, 1990.

_____. *Parabola, Journal of Myth and Tradition*. "Dreams and Seeing," VII, no. 2, 1982.

Mattoon, Mary Ann. *Understanding Dreams*. Dallas: Spring Publications, 1978.

Meade, Michael. *Men and the Water of Life: Initiation and the Tempering of Men*. San Francisco: Harper, 1993.

Thomas Moore. *Parabola, Journal of Myth and Tradition*. "The Soul's Religion," xxi, 2 1996.

Morris, Robert. *WEAVINGS*. "New Clothes for the Soul," Jan-Feb 96.

Progoff, Ira. *The Practice of Process Meditation*. New York: Dialogue House Library, 1980.

Raffa, Jean Benedict, Ed.D. *Dream Theatres of the Soul*. San Diego: LuraMedia, 1994.

Reed, Henry, Ph.D. *Awaking Your Psychic Powers*. San Francisco: Harper and Row, 1988. Reprinted by St. Martins Press, 1998.
_____. *Dream Solutions*. Virginia Beach: Inner Vision, 1993. Sixth edition now available as *Dream Solutions, Dream Realizations: Obtaining Intuitive Guidance From Dreams*, Mouth of Wilson, Virginia: Hermes Home Press (www.creativespirit.net/henryreed/hermeshomepress)

_____. *Getting Help From Your Dreams*. New York: Ballantine Books, 1985. Mouth of Wilson, Virginia: Hermes Home Press (www.creativespirit.net/henryreed/hermeshomepress)

Roberts, Susan B. *Common Boundary: Between Spirituality and Psychotherapy*. "The Soul of the World: Exploring Archetypal Psychology," Nov-Dec, 1992.

_____. *Common Boundary: Between Spirituality and Psychotherapy*. "Finding Soul in Everyday Life, An Interview with Thomas Moore," Nov-Dec, 1992.

Savary, Louis, Berne, Patricia, and Williams, Strephon. *Dreams and Spiritual Growth: A Judaeo-Christian Approach to Spirituality*. New York: Paulist Press, 1984.

Singer, June. *Boundaries of the Soul*. Garden City, NJ: Anchor Books, 1973.

Taylor, Jeremy. *Dream Work: Techniques for Discovering the Creative Power in Dreams*. New York: Paulist Press, 1983.

Williams, Strephon Kaplan. *Jungian-Senoi Dreamwork Manual*. Berkeley: Journey Press, 1980.

Winson, Jonathan. *Scientific American*. "The Meaning of Dreams." November 1990: 86-96.

Zinker, Joseph. *Creative Process in Gestalt Therapy*. New York: Vintage Books, 1978.

B. Bibliography of Carl G. Jung References

Carl G. Jung. *Man and His Symbols*. Garden City: Doubleday, 1964.

_____. *Memories, Dreams, and Reflections*. New York: Pantheon,1963.

Read, Sir Herbert, et al, Ed. *Collected Works of Carl G. Jung, Bollingen Series*. New York: Princeton University Press, 1970:

_____. *Freud and Psychoanalysis*. "The Significance of the Father in the Destiny of the Individual," v. 4.

_____. *Two Essays on Analytical Psychology*. "On the Psychology of the Unconscious," "The Relations Between the Ego and the Unconscious," v. 7.

_____. *The Archetypes and the Collective Unconscious*. "Psychological Aspects of the Mother Archetype,""The Psychology of the Child Archetype," "The Phenomenology of the Spirit in Fairy Tales," "Conscious, Unconscious, and Individuation," "Concerning Mandala Symbolism," v. 9.i.

_____. *Aion.: Researches into the Phenomenology of the Self*, "The Ego," "The Shadow," "The Syzgy: Anima and Animus," v. 9.ii, 3-22.

_____. *Civilization in Transition*. "The Undiscovered Self (Present and Future)," v. 10.

_____. *Psychology and Alchemy*. "Individual Dream Symbolism in Relation to Alchemy," "Religious Ideas in Alchemy," v. 12.

_____. *Mysterium Coniunctionis*. "Personification of the Opposites,"v. 14.

_____. *The Symbolic Life*. "The Tavistock Lectures, Lecture V," "Symbols and the Interpretation of Dreams," v. 18.

C. Bibliography For Collective Dreaming

Campbell, Joseph with Moyers, Boll. *The Power of Myth*. New York: Doubleday, 1988.

Dombeck, Mary-Therese Behar, R.N., D.Min. *Journal of Psychiatry* (University of Ottawa). "Group Mythology and Group Development in Dream Sharing groups," 13, no.2, (1988): 97-106.

Jobes, Gertrude. *Dictionary of Mythology, Folklore, and Symbols*. New York: Scarecrow Press, 1972.

Jung, C.G. *The Collected Works of Carl G. Jung*. Edited by Sir Herbert Read, et al. 20 volumes. Bollingen Series. New York: Princeton University Press, 1970. [See separate bibliography of Jungian references.]

Neihardt, John G. *Black Elk Speaks*. New York: Pocket Books, 1972.

Reed, Henry, Ph.D. *The Community Sundance Journal*. "The Sundance Experiment: I An Introduction," 1, no.1 (1976) 108-141.

_____. *The Community Sundance Journal*. "The Sundance Experiment: II Images of the Motif," 1, no. 2 (1877) 258-281.

_____. *The Community Sundance Journal*. "The Sundance Experiment: III The Dialogue Between the Unconscious and Society," 2, no. 1 (1978) 121-139.

_____. *The Community Sundance Journal*. "The Sundance Experiment: IV

Dreaming Together," 2, no.2 (1978) 264-281.

_____. *The Community Sundance Journal.* "The Sundance Experiment: V Subscribers' Dream About Sundance," 3, no.1 (1979) 1331-139

_____. *The Community Sundance Journal.* "The Sundance Experiment: VI The Dancers," 2. no.2 (Summer, 1979) 109-125.

Rohr, Richard. *SPIRIT, SOUL & SOCIETY.* Kansas City: Credence Cassettes, 1993.

Shipler, David. *Arab and Jew: Wounded Spirits in a Promised Land.* New York: Times Books, 1992.

Watkins, Susan M. *Dreaming Myself, Dreaming a Town.* New York: Kendall Enterprises, 1989.

PROCESS GUIDELINES FOR COMMUNAL DREAM WORK

CALENDAR FOR "TRIBAL" DREAM CHAPTER
Sisters of Saint Joseph of Nazareth

REMOTE PREPARATION

An invitation was presented to Sister Pat Brockman, OSU, in the early
summer of 1993 to assist in the preparation for Chapter, 1994, by collecting the
"tribal" dreams of the Congregation. Pat submitted a formal proposal to the
Chapter Facilitating Committee on August 24, 1993.

+ Acceptance came through Sister Rose Cadaret, SSJ, on September 28, 1993,
along with a sub-committee to work on dream logistics: Joyce Dropps, Lucy
Schneider, Mary Rita Sayers, and Rose Cadaret.

+ Letter of invitation, registration forms, tapes ready to go out in early January

+ The afternoon of April 10, 1994, 1:00-4:00 pm

FACILITATORS TRAINING DAY. How many?

+ Saturday, April 23, Detroit Discernment Day

+ Sunday, April 24, Nazareth Discernment Day

+ Final Presentation to Chapter will only be a portion of the day—amount of time
to be discerned.

DIRECT PREPARATION

1. By the middle of December, Pat will have provided a letter of invitation and an
audiotape presenting the "significance and foundation of community dreaming."

    A. <u>This will include</u>:

      a) some Jungian background;

      b) a description and foundation of the project;

      c) the format for the dream work/play;

      d) encouragement to stay in the process; and,

      e) a calendar as well as a deadline for submitting dreams to be used for
Chapter.

    B. <u>Each focus group will listen to the tape together</u>.

2. March 18-19, DREAM NIGHT! Deadline for sending a copy of <u>any</u> dream: ASAP,
or up until March 25.

3. Sunday, April 10, Training of Dream Facilitators

<u>Goal of meeting</u>: To prepare a group of sisters to lead the discernment processes.

4. Discernment Days (April 23 and 24)

<u>Goal of these days</u>: To identify in the dreams common themes or patterns or unique
images; to reflect on and name their significance to the charism, history, current
issues and future directions of the SSJs.

5. Saturday, July 23, 1994, <u>Chapter Day</u>

JOSEPH THE DREAMER TOWARD A NEW CREATION!

INTRODUCTION AND BACKGROUND

Sisters, those who study religious life are proposing a modification in the way religious congregations carry out their Chapter work. Religious women - drawing on their gifts to discern and reorganize the serious tasks of renewal - have accomplished massive amounts of adaptation, restructuring, and lifestyle change.

Many, however, desire a fresh use of their meeting and planning time. They have often found that in the renewal process it is moments of common prayer, grief over a treasured loss, or shared rituals which have been the source of deepest bonding among them. It is the place of mystery and call which has frequently been inexplicable, yet most powerful.

At the same time, returning to the mysticism of early Christians, it is the realm of the dream that is increasingly being restored to our prayer and practice. The scriptural experience of Old Testament dreams give us a model in a <u>listening</u> Joseph (Gen 31, 47), a <u>wrestling</u> Jacob (Gen 28:10-22), and a <u>prophetic</u> Daniel (Dan 2:27ff). The New Testament, too, reveals the <u>humble response</u> of Joseph, father of Jesus, living out God's message given to the Beloved in sleep (Matt 1:18-2:15).

Listening, wrestling, prophetic, and humble response! The qualities of these dreamers speak to the current experience of many religious. It is my proposal that religious men and women again develop the discipline and the art of dreaming, not just for themselves, but for their communities. This involves an interweaving process of praying, collecting dreams, communal discernment of their meaning and - from the discernment - identification of areas for group growth or action.

The long term purpose of being attentive to God's word in community dreams is

TRANSFORMATION, or CONVERSION

<u>*not only of individuals, but of the Congregation and of the Church*</u>.

Therefore, dreams are approached as a faith experience and as prayer.

DESCRIPTION AND FOUNDATION OF THE PROJECT

So you are invited to join in listening for God's word in your dreams, to ask God to speak to the Sisters of Saint Joseph of Nazareth <u>as a Congregation</u>, to believe that God will speak to you as He did to the prophets about Israel. The night chosen, Saint Joseph's feast, appropriately acknowledges your great saint connecting you to the charism and spirit which he has inspired.

The overall information in the form of this written material and tape is directed to three things: (1) pointing to helpful scriptural and psychological background; (2) describing the project itself; and (3) giving a format for steps of the dream experience.

<u>Your</u> participation is significant. In fact, the point is to bring to the community discernment <u>your</u> aspect of the shared life. The Community is comprised of separate and unique individuals, but together you make up the community. <u>Together</u> your dreams describe the "collective soul" of the Body of Christ which is the Sisters of Saint Joseph of Nazareth. Each Sister who participates makes the message of God clearer to the group.

There are basically five steps:
1. <u>Preparation</u> by prayer and reflection on the current movement of the Spirit among you and your desire to hear God's call.

2. Joining with your sisters in <u>asking for a Congregational dream</u> on the night of March 18-19. Submitting any dreams received as soon as possible, <u>no later</u> than April 10.

3. <u>Facilitators Day</u>: A training day for the sisters who will be facilitating the April 23/24 Discernment Days and the Chapter Dream process. The role of the facilitators will be to assist members in reaching an understanding of the dream messages.

4. <u>Days of Discernment of Dreams</u>: Any and all sisters who wish to attend are welcome. As the trained dream "organizer," Sister Pat can design and assist the process, and the facilitators can direct the meetings, but <u>you</u> are the ones who know best the heart of your congregational charism. These will be days of <u>playing and working</u> with the dreams!

    * Time will include (1) prayer, (2) teaching, (3) reflection, and (4) small group work. Facilitators will be directing the discernment in small groups. Themes and common images of the SSJ charism, history, and current issues

will be identified from dream symbols. These patterns will provide a base for describing at Chapter (a) the Congregation's "soul," (b) its underlying questions, and (c) possible future directions.

* Project Director (Sister Pat Brockman) will collect and organize the themes which surface on Discernment Days. Her purpose will be to arrange them in coherent form for Chapter discussion. A complete copy of the dreams and themes will be made available to all for future reference.

5. What happens in the Chapter Experience?

THE SISTERS WILL APPLY THEMES OF THE DREAMS

TO QUESTIONS AND CONCERNS WHICH CONFRONT THE CHAPTER.

This means that the Sisters <u>as a Body</u> hear God's word, accept its communally understood meaning, and decide what kind of recognition or action is appropriate.

SOME COMMON QUESTIONS, LIKE: WHAT DO I DO NEXT, HOW DO I KNOW THIS IS A COMMUNITY DREAM...?

* What you do next is ask for a dream for March 18-19.
* <u>Record it before it fades</u>. Give it a title - it's *your* parable of the Congregation!
* Mail your copy to Sister Pat on the form provided.
* Feel free to make comments on the meaning of the dream. What is it trying to tell us?

Think of it as a "tribal" dream! In all traditions, especially our Judeo-Christian one, devout people have believed that God speaks to his/her people in dreams. Today psychology explores and supports the word of God in dreams. Carl Jung "discovered" that there is not just a universal soul or individual soul, but each nation, group, family has a collective soul. How much more likely those who are committed to hearing God together!

Some Guidelines

1. The GOAL of the dream is transformation, or conversion, of the person and/or of the community.

2. Dreams are a product of the unconscious, or inner reality. They come from the same place as that of our prayer and prayer images. Dreamwork becomes just a fad (like prayer) IF it is not related to our outer reality of relationship and ministry.

3. There are many layers of meaning in dreams: healing, telepathic, archetypal, past-oriented, prophetic, health, COMMUNITY....

4. A common way to play with an image is to confront it: name it, describe it, ask its significance, and dialogue with it.

5. Journalizing is an essential discipline in dreamwork. The dream or vision must be written down. Association with something familiar is a chief way to raise awareness of the dream's meaning. The most helpful approaches are imaginative or non-rational, e.g., playful approaches such as drawing, writing rhymes, or fantasizing, or acting out the dream or its images.

The images are NOT LITERAL, BUT SYMBOLIC, so please do not pre-judge your dream as good or bad. Refrain from saying it's too bizarre <u>or</u> too ordinary to be useful! The dream will use human images to express a message, including such earthy symbols as sexual or bathroom images, or the large experiences of humanity such as war or birth. But the image is symbolic of a larger reality which you will extract in due time. Send the dream even if you can't understand it.

In Pat Brockman's thirty years work with religiously-oriented communities, she has been privy to, and challenged by, the tension between the individual and institutional souls. Her book enters into this tension with original experiments, using the community dreams of persons who cooperate intentionally. She finds that these common dreams and images act as transforming symbols in the communal life. As an Ursuline Sister of Brown County, Ohio, and a founding member of New Jerusalem Community, Cincinnati, Ohio, she has held leadership positions that include community development, pastoral counseling, and administration.

In these roles she has worked extensively with Carl Jung's personality types and his archetypal concepts, facilitating group process and community building among religious, educational, and business enterprises. She is currently a presenter on dream interpretation and spirituality. This work has taken her to groups across the United States and Canada, including religious sisters, families, gay men, hospital executives and administrators, as well as parishes, lay communities, and dream-sharing groups. Grounded in Jung's concept of the collective psyche, Dr. Brockman specializes in leading these various communities to identify and collect their own tribal dreams.

Pat Brockman is certified by the Cincinnati Gestalt Institute, Cincinnati, Ohio, and in spiritual direction by the Jesuit Renewal Center in Milford, Ohio. She is a community consultant, retreat director, and personal spiritual advisor. She received her Ph.D. in Community Psychology from the Union Institute in Cincinnati, Ohio, and has studied at the C.G. Jung Institute in Zurich, Switzerland.

Publications include:

Dreams Transform Our Lives, 4 cassettes, Kansas City: Credence Cassettes, 1996. [Now Credence Communications.]

Human Development, "A Community's Tribal Dreams," v. 16, no. 2, Summer, 1995.

Richard Rohr: Illuminations of His Life and Work, New York: Crossroad, 1993. (Andreas Ebert and Patricia Brockman, editors.)

Praying, "The Five Hopeful Mysteries," October, 1989. Reprinted in *The Catholic Digest*.

For more Information, or to obtain copies of this book, contact:

Pat C. Brockman, O.S.U., Ph.D.
763 McMakin Avenue
Cincinnati, Ohio 45232
513-541-4559
pcb@fuse.net

or
WovenWord Press
811 Mapleton Avenue
Boulder Colorado 80304
888 773 7738
books@wovenword.com
www.wovenword.com